Dear Church

The Letters To The Seven Churches Of Asia

A Lenten Bible Study

Bill Thomas

CSS Publishing Company, Inc.
Lima, Ohio

DEAR CHURCH

FIRST EDITION
Copyright © 2021
by CSS Publishing Co., Inc.

Library of Congress Cataloging-in-Publication Data

 Names: Thomas, Bill, 1965- author. Title: Dear church : the letters to the seven churches of Asia / Bill   Thomas. Description: First edition. | Lima, Ohio : CSS Publishing Company, Inc.,   [2021] | "A Lenten Bible study." Identifiers: LCCN 2021019759 | ISBN 9780788030444 (paperback) | ISBN   9780788030451 (ebook) Subjects: LCSH: Bible. Revelation, I-III--Criticism, interpretation, etc. | Bible. Revelation, I-III--Textbooks. Classification: LCC BS2825.52 .T4595 2021 | DDC 228/.06--dc23 LC record available at https://lccn.loc.gov/2021019759

For more information about CSS Publishing Company resources, visit our website at www. csspub.com, email us at csr@csspub.com, or call (800) 241-4056.

e-book:
ISBN-13: 978-0-7880-3045-1
ISBN-10: 0-7880-3045-0

ISBN-13: 978-0-7880-3044-4
ISBN-10: 0-7880-3044-2

ELECTRONICALLY PRINTED

Acknowledgements

Thanks to the following people who helped make this book possible:

David Runk, Karyl Corson and their team at CSS Publishing. They are an amazing group to work with and are committed to helping churches. It is an honor to serve with you.

Dottie Bodewitz and Dave Smith at First Christian Church in Washington, MO. Dottie is one of the best at proofreading and Dave shared great insights into these lessons.

Those who attend First Christian Church in Washington, MO and the staff with whom I am blessed to work. These lessons were originally a series of life group lessons that we shared together.

The Alpha and Omega, Our Lord Jesus Christ. Without him, there is no church. To him be glory forever, Amen.

Contents

Introduction

I've written some Easter Bible studies before, but I am confident that this one is unique. It's an Easter study on the first few chapters of Revelation. I'm guessing that's not a part of the Bible you've connected with Easter before, but I think there's an important message in that text. Most Easter studies end with the resurrection of Jesus Christ, but that's where this study begins. It starts with a look at the glorious picture of the Lord in Revelation 1 and then focuses on his message to his church.

Jesus Christ said to Peter after Peter's confession, "And I tell you that you are Peter, and on this rock I will build my church, and the gates of Hades will not overcome it" (Matthew 16:18). The church has been a powerful force for proclaiming the gospel message and reaching the lost, hurting, and broken with the love of Jesus Christ. Generations of people have come to know Jesus Christ and lived for him because the church has fulfilled her mission to "Therefore go and make disciples of all nations, baptizing them in the name of the Father and of the Son and of the Holy Spirit, and teaching them to obey everything I have commanded you. And surely I am with you always, to the very end of the age" (Matthew 28:19-20).

We can celebrate that, in 2018, there were 2.3 billion people who claimed to be Christians around the world.[1] Church organizations across the spectrum of denominations are working to help solve world hunger. Missionaries continue to take the gospel of Jesus Christ across the globe. There are a lot of things right about the church.

However, the church is facing some challenges. The church's influence in culture seems to be less than it ever has been.[2] Church attendance across denominations and across the United States is down and a 2019 Gallup Report suggested that only half of

1 "10 Church Statistics You Need To Know For 2018", Reach Right. https://reachrightstudios.com/10-church-statistics-need-know-2018/.
2 Joe Carter, "Why do Millennials Consider the Church a Negative Influence on Society?" The Gospel Coalition, January 5, 2016. https://www.thegospelcoalition.org/article/why-do-millennials-consider-the-church-a-negative-influence-on-society/.

Dear Church

Americans are church members, down from 70% in 1999.

It seems to me the church is in a battle. It's a struggle to continue her eternal purpose; carry on her calling; and maintain relevance in a world that is changing rapidly. There are many books and lots of teaching material on how the church can stay relevant. I don't pretend that this book is the ultimate answer to those perplexing challenges. It does seem to me, though, that the church's struggle today isn't all that different from the difficulties the church faced in the first century. That's the reason for this book.

The seven churches of Asia, addressed in Revelation 2 and 3, were dealing with many of the same issues that torment the church today. I understand that when we delve into the book of Revelation, it can be tough. I'm guessing there are more books about Revelation than any other book of the Bible. People discuss and debate the meaning of the last book of the Bible regularly. However, if we look at the seven churches of Asia as real churches with real people, I believe there's a lot we can learn from them. That's my prayer, anyway.

This Easter, see Jesus Christ as you haven't before and consider his message to you and your church. May your passion for serving him be rekindled. May your love for him and others grow. May your faith increase. Let's give him all we have until the day we can hear the blessed words, "Well done, my good and faithful servant" (Matthew 25:21).

Before You Begin Notes

Before you use this book for personal or group study, there are some things you need to know.

> 1. In this study we'll look at the seven churches as real churches with real people. I know there are some who want to see them as a type of church throughout history. Others want to combine both approaches, seeing the churches in history and as a type. This study doesn't take that approach. We're considering what was written to them in the time they lived.

2.   This study does not take an interpretive view of Revelation. Whether you are a millennial, pre-millennial or post-millennial, this study can be of help to you.

3.   This study can be done in a group setting or for an individual Bible study.

How To Use This Study

If the book is being done in an individual study, the reader can go through each lesson and consider the discussion questions at the end of each chapter.

If the book is being done in a group setting, the whole group can read through or summarize the lesson and discuss the questions at the end of each chapter. There are nine chapters, which could easily be done in a nine-week study. The lessons are written to last between sixty and ninety minutes.

Personal Note

I want to thank you for getting this book and I pray that it will be a catalyst for Jesus Christ, the Alpha and Omega, to share a message that will impact you and your church. May Jesus Christ inspire, challenge, and bless you, always.

— Bill Thomas

Lesson 1

Who Is This?

Revelation is one of the most discussed and written about books in the Bible. Is it a book of prophecy about the future? Is it a record of the church's persecution in the first century? Is it a combination of both? Martin Lloyd Jones said of Revelation, "Though terribly misunderstood today, it is a fascinating book intended for the encouragement of the church."[3]

The focus of Revelation isn't to allow readers to pinpoint the day of Christ's return, nor is it to generate debate and discussion about the particulars of the end times. The central thrust of the book, and this study, is to encourage Christians. The message resonated at the end of the first century, and I believe the message resonates today, too.

This book focuses on the letters to the seven churches. In a time when the church is struggling to maintain relevance in a challenging culture, the letters to the seven churches in Asia carry important messages. When young people today are questioning whether the church and the Christian faith are real, these letters address genuine faith. When our skeptical culture demands that we show our faith, these letters address what faith looks like. A look at the letters to the seven churches can be a refreshing way to increase our faith and demonstrate to the world around us that we follow Jesus Christ.

Before we get to the substance of the letters, though, we ought to spend a little time looking at the one the letters are from, the Lord Jesus Christ. The Christ we see in Revelation 1 is different than the usual "Sunday school" look at him. Here's the text.

Revelation 1:7-8 and 12-20

[7]Look! He comes with the clouds of heaven. And

3 Brian Hedges, "Quotes and Resources on the Book of Revelation", Brian Hedges (blog), August 7, 2010. http://www.brianghedges.com/2010/08/quotes-and-resources-on-book-of.html.

everyone will see him — even those who pierced him. And all the nations of the world will mourn for him. Yes! Amen!

8 "I am the Alpha and the Omega — the beginning and the end," says the Lord God. "I am the one who is, who always was, and who is still to come — the Almighty One."

12When I turned to see who was speaking to me, I saw seven gold lampstands. 13And standing in the middle of the lampstands was someone like the Son of Man. He was wearing a long robe with a gold sash across his chest. 14His head and his hair were white like wool, as white as snow. And his eyes were like flames of fire. 15His feet were like polished bronze refined in a furnace, and his voice thundered like mighty ocean waves. 16He held seven stars in his right hand, and a sharp two-edged sword came from his mouth. And his face was like the sun in all its brilliance.

17When I saw him, I fell at his feet as if I were dead. But he laid his right hand on me and said, "Don't be afraid! I am the First and the Last. 18I am the living one. I died, but look — I am alive forever and ever! And I hold the keys of death and the grave.

19"Write down what you have seen — both the things that are now happening and the things that will happen. 20This is the meaning of the mystery of the seven stars you saw in my right hand and the seven gold lampstands: The seven stars are the angels of the seven churches, and the seven lampstands are the seven churches.(Revelation 1:7-8, 12-20 NLT)

Seeing Jesus Christ has always been important. John 12:21 records for us that some Greeks came to Philip with a simple request. They said, "Sir, we want to see Jesus." (John 12:21 NRSV) That's really the desire of every Christian's heart, isn't it? More than anything else, we want to see Jesus Christ. There's something in us that yearns to see our Savior.

Helen Howarth Lemmel captured that feeling in her hymn, "The Heavenly Vision." She wrote in the first verse and chorus these words of hope.

> *O soul, are you weary and troubled?*
> *No light in the darkness you see.*
> *There's light for a look at the Savior,*
> *And life more abundant and free!*
> *Turn your eyes upon Jesus,*
> *Look full in His wonderful face,*
> *And the things of earth will grow strangely dim,*
> *In the light of His glory and grace.* [4]

In the first chapter of Revelation, John provides a rich description of the one from whom he received a revelation. It is an introduction that can't be forgotten.

Introductions matter because they create an impression. Did you know that there is a proper way to introduce someone notable or famous who's about to speak to your group? I found multiple websites and guides that can help people learn how to make a proper introduction. The best tip is to ask the speaker if they have an introduction they want you to use. Most public speakers or keynote speakers will have an introduction already prepared. Just stick to the script and you and your speaker will both come off looking like rock stars.[5]

When an introduction goes badly, it can be awkward. Consider Bobbe White's story. Bobbe White is a motivational speaker from Illinois. She's been around a while which led to an interesting introduction. She described it this way:

"When speaking in St. Louis, the emcee introduced me

---

4 Lemell, Helen Howarth, "The Heavenly Vison," God tube, https://www.god tube.com/popular-hymns/the-heavenly-vision-turn-your-eyes-upon-jesus-/,
5 Michael Nichols, "How to Introduce a Keynote Speaker Without Embarrassing Yourself", Michael Nichols: Leadership Made Simple (blog). https://michaelnichols.org/introduce-keynote-speaker/.

this way: 'Let's give a warm welcome to Bobbe Whitehair!' The audience roared! That is, until they realized the emcee's embarrassment and thought I might have been offended. Well, his face was turning multiple shades of red. Me? I was laughing because it was funny! And quite accurate. A speaker's goal is to get a laugh within the first fifteen seconds. His faux pas certainly did, and it broke the ice in a good way.

I now have written into my introduction: "Let's give a warm welcome to a woman whose hair matches her name.... Bobbe White!" I explain the introduction incident and it helps deliver my first point: laugh at your own expense!"[6]

I like that story. It highlights for us how important introductions are. In this first lesson, we are introduced to one who is the central figure for this study and all of history. Let's dig in.

Lesson

Although many people assume that Revelation is all about the end of the world, it is primarily a look at Jesus Christ, who is present among the churches and active in the affairs of humanity. From the view of the Lord himself, chapters 2-3 of Revelation look at what was going on in the seven churches. The identity of Christ is explained dramatically in the first chapter. He's one worthy of being heard. To begin, let's look at how he is described.

Who Is He?

> 1. Powerful
> We are first made aware of his incredible power. The Greek word translated Revelation is apokalupsis (apocalypse). The word simply means "a revealing, an unveiling." What does the book of Revelation reveal? It is the Revelation of Jesus Christ in two distinct ways. This book is Jesus Christ's Revelation in the sense that it belongs to him. He was the one doing the revealing. It is also Jesus' Revelation in the sense that he is the object

6 White, Bobbe, "Try Laughter! Inc, http://www.trylaughter.com/index.html

revealed; Jesus Christ was the person revealed by the book.

In verse five, we find Jesus was "the faithful witness, the firstborn from the dead, and the ruler of the kings of the earth." Jesus "loves us and freed us from our sins by his blood" (v.5) and, by doing so, he was a "faithful witness."The Greek word for witness is the root word from which the English word "martyr" derives. The fact that Jesus Christ is the "firstborn from the dead" does not indicate that he is a created being, but is a statement of prominence. Those who have a relationship with him will follow in his resurrection to life. He was also the ruler of the kings of the earth. There was no one greater than the one who was appearing to John and was giving him this message.

In Revelation 1:7 we see a quote from Daniel 7 and Zechariah 12. John Gill wrote, "The manner of his coming will be "with clouds"; either figuratively, with angels, who will attend him both for grandeur and service, or literally, in the clouds of heaven; he shall descend in like manner as he ascended, and as Daniel prophesied he should, (Daniel 7:13)."[7] Jesus Christ is coming "with the clouds." In the Old Testament, this imagery is used when God is coming in judgment and indicates his incredible power.

What John beheld here as the Revelation began to unfold was the remarkable power of Jesus Christ. This appearance was in stark contrast to the Messiah's first appearance. Then, he came as "a baby wrapped in cloths and lying in a manger" (Luke 2:12 NRSV). Now, though, John and the whole world saw the incredible power of Jesus Christ.

7 Gill, John, Gill's Exposition of the Bible, Revelation 1, https://www.biblestudytools.com/commentaries/gills-exposition-of-the-bible-revelation-1-7.html

Revelation 1:8 is also an important verse in looking at the Christ. In Revelation 1:8, Jesus said of himself, "I am the Alpha and the Omega," says the Lord God, "who is, and who was, and who is to come, the Almighty." In his own words, we see Jesus Christ declaring his sovereignty. He noted the first and last letters of the Greek alphabet, alpha and omega, to indicate he was in control of history from beginning to end.

Jesus Christ's power is vividly seen in this introduction. Do you know his power?

2. I had the chance to work in our church's fair booth where we make potato chips and "tornado potatoes." I know that sounds harsh, but, trust me, they're good. We offered cheese and chili with them. I opened the booth early one morning and my volunteer crew arrived. I'd already put the chili in the crockpots, and we were ready to open.

After we'd used about half of the first crockpot, one of the volunteers checked to see how warm the chili in the second pot was. He was startled that it was still cold. How could that be? It had been in there over an hour. We were both puzzled and wondered if the crockpot was broken, until we discovered the truth… it wasn't plugged in. No power.

Power was at our disposal, but our chili was cold. Why? We didn't use it. With electricity, that's just crazy. With Jesus Christ, though, it is tragic. Revelation 1 indicates he is powerful.

3. Glorious
The second attribute of the Christ that we see in this first chapter is his amazing glory. Revelation 1:12-13 describe Jesus Christ as standing in the middle of seven

lampstands. He's also called "someone like the Son of Man." The lampstands, we learn, are the seven churches (v.20). We'll look at them more closely later. There is, though, a reference that we shouldn't miss. The phrase "Son of Man" is a messianic title which Jesus used a lot to describe himself in the gospels. It's a statement that reflects his incarnation. Jesus Christ is God in the flesh. In this chapter, his glory is fully displayed.

Verses 14-15 reverberate with his glory. Catch these words. "The hair on his head was white like wool, as white as snow, and his eyes were like blazing fire. His feet were like bronze glowing in a furnace, and his voice was like the sound of rushing waters."

His white hair was not so much a representation of age as it is a symbol of his glory. It was likely connected to him being the "Ancient of Days" (see Daniel 7:9). His eyes were described as a "blazing fire." It's an awesome description that speaks of God's appearance as we see in Ezekiel 1:27, Daniel 10:6 and here proclaimed Jesus Christ's knowledge and grace in purifying souls. Jesus Christ can search and penetrate the hearts of all men. His glory and divine nature are revealed as the Revelation begins. The description of his feet indicates his ability to care for and support his people. His voice reverberates like rushing waters. This picture of Christ radiates his glory.

Verse 16 says, "In his right hand he held seven stars, and coming out of his mouth was a sharp, double-edged sword. His face was like the sun shining in all its brilliance." The seven stars likely represent the seven churches. The sharp, double-edged sword is a reference to the Word of God (see Ephesians 6:17 and Hebrews 4:12). It comes out of Jesus' mouth and rebukes sin. It's also a powerful convicting agent. The description of his face speaks majestically of his glory and splendor. The word is used so much today, but in this passage Jesus Christ is truly awesome.

Jesus Christ's glory, though, can be minimized or ignored. I don't think it is intentional, but sometimes our walk with the Lord becomes routine. Being in his presence no longer thrills us like it used to do. It wasn't that way for John. When he saw all this, he fell at his feet as though he was dead (v. 17). Seeing Jesus Christ this way touched John in a profound way. He was awed. When was the last time you were awed by something?

I read about Nick Noah of Urbandale, Iowa in "The Des Moines Register." On Christmas Day, 2018, Noah saw bright colors for the first time.

Noah had been color vision deficient his entire life; only able to see dull, "worn down" shades. Standing in the backyard, he put on "color blind glasses," a surprise gift from his dad, and walked toward a row of rainbow balloons taped to the deck. He was speechless.

Noah said, "There are no words to describe it other than life-changing. It was easily the most overwhelmed I have ever been."[8]

May you be awed and overwhelmed in the presence of your life-changing Savior.

4. Victorious

The chapter concludes with an astounding depiction of

---

8 Shelby Flieg, "A 'life-changing' Christmas Gift: Iowa Man's Reaction to 'color blind glasses' Goes Viral", The Des Moines Register, January 3, 2018. https://www.desmoinesregister.com/story/news/2019/01/03/color-blind-iowa-man-enchroma-glasses-twitter-vision-deficient-urbandale-ia-video-christmas-day/2471883002/.

Jesus Christ as the victor. Of all the descriptions of the Christ, this one might resonate more than any other. The book of Revelation reveals some difficult times for the church. Christians throughout history and around the world have known persecution. On a personal level, we likely know what it means to struggle.

Is there any of us that hasn't felt the sting of betrayal, disappointment, or discouragement? If you've stood by a casket at a visitation; if you've knelt to pray beside a sickbed; if you've spent countless lonely hours alone waiting for the right someone; if you've added and re-added the numbers and find what's owed is more than what's in the bank; if you've been stuck in a job you hate with people who don't respect you; if you've heard the words "I don't love you anymore;" or if you've grown up without a parent or one who was far less than what they ought to have been, there's news for you. Jesus has won the victory, his and yours.

In verse 17 we read, "When I saw him, I fell at his feet as though dead. Then he placed his right hand on me and said: "Do not be afraid. I am the First and the Last. I am the Living One; I was dead, and now look, I am alive for ever and ever! And I hold the keys of death and Hades."

Jesus Christ is the victorious conqueror. It isn't surprising that John fell at his feet. Notice, too, what he told John in his own introduction. He called himself, "the First and the Last" and "the Living One." He declared, "I was dead, and now look, I am alive for ever and ever!" Not only that, he had the keys of death and Hades.

The "First and Last" statement connects with the "Alpha and Omega" reference made earlier and denotes his sovereignty. It's also a way to alleviate John's fear (see Isaiah 41:4). Jesus Christ is, was, and will always be. He is

19

Lord of everything.

Jesus Christ's victory over death and the grave is also highlighted. The statement "I am alive for ever and ever" is a shout of triumph. Is there any more important declaration in human history? In the life and death battle of sin for the souls of men, Jesus Christ triumphed over Satan, destroying the power of both death and the grave. He now holds the keys of death and Hades as tokens of that victory. Because of Jesus Christ, you and I can have victory, too.

E.M. Bartlett described that in a hymn in 1939. He wrote:

> *O victory in Jesus,*
> *My Savior, forever.*
> *He sought me and bought me*
> *With His redeeming blood;*
> *He loved me ere I knew Him*
> *And all my love is due Him,*
> *He plunged me to victory,*
> *Beneath the cleansing flood.*[9]

I'm a baseball fan. I'm also a fan of the Kansas City Royals. For those of you who don't know baseball, being a Royals fan can be a bit tough. The Royals won the World Series in 1985 and then had a 29-year playoff drought. In 2014, the Royals earned a wild card spot and played the Oakland A's on September 30. The game was one of the most exciting I've ever watched. The game was four hours and 45 minutes long, twelve innings and the Royals came from behind twice to win 9-8. When Salvador Perez drove in Christian Colon, the Royals had a victory. I can still remember the excitement I felt over that win. Finally, after almost three decades, the Royals were winners. A World Series was ahead for that team and a World Series win the next year.

While those wins were exciting, I still remember the wild card game. Victory after so many years of losing.

Victories are sweet. We all know that. Sports wins are good, but nothing compares to the victory we have in Jesus. The grave no longer needs to be feared. Life wins. The things of this world that would try to hold you down drop powerless beside you. Hate, anger, and fear have no place as love wins. What Paul wrote in Romans 8:35-39 echoes across time.

> [35]Who shall separate us from the love of Christ? Shall trouble or hardship or persecution or famine or nakedness or danger or sword? [36]As it is written:
>
> "For your sake we face death all day long; we are considered as sheep to be slaughtered."
>
> [37]No, in all these things we are more than conquerors through him who loved us. [38]For I am convinced that neither death nor life, neither angels nor demons, neither the present nor the future, nor any powers, [39]neither height nor depth, nor anything else in all creation, will be able to separate us from the love of God that is in Christ Jesus our Lord.

Because of Jesus Christ, you and I are victorious.

Discussion Questions

1. When you think of Jesus Christ, what comes to mind? What are some words you might use to describe him?

2. Revelation verses 7 and 8 talk about how all will see him and acknowledge who he is and what he's done (what they've done to him). In what ways does your life, right now, recognize or acknowledge Jesus?

3. The book of Revelation, which is often viewed as a prophetic book, begins with a clear introduction

of Jesus. He's called the "Alpha" and "Omega", or the beginning and the end. What does it mean to all humanity that history begins and ends with Jesus? Jesus Christ is the focal point of all history. Is he the focal point of your life? Your family? Your church? How?

4. We've heard it said that all we do is to be done for Jesus. What are some struggles that you have in making that happen? What might help you live more easily or clearly for Jesus?

5. Jesus is called in this text the "Son of Man." That's a term that's found in the gospels quite a bit. The title touches on the incarnation. In what ways does it matter that Jesus was fully human as you are?

6. Jesus Christ tells John that he holds the keys to death and the grave. That's a powerful statement from the resurrected Jesus. Why do you think so many people fear death? Should a Christian? Do you? Why or why not?

7. I can't help but see Jesus' power when I read these verses. His voice, his eyes, his feet, and his face all radiate his incredible power. Why do I struggle to allow him and his amazing power to work in my life?

8. What does Jesus' victory mean for you? How does it impact your life?

Prayer Focus: Pray that you might see who Jesus is and to be able to contemplate what he means to you so that you can more fully give your life to him.

Lesson 2

Letter To The Church At Ephesus
Love Grown Cold

Being passionate for Jesus Christ and his mission is the desire of every church. No church simply decides that they want to be irrelevant to their community or ineffective. The truth is, though, some churches do lose their passion. Their zeal for the Lord gives way to going through the motions. Perhaps that's a story you've seen play out. It was the story of the church at Ephesus. Jesus Christ challenged them and us in a practical way.

As we launch this study, we need to recognize who these churches are. Some assert that the seven churches are representative of seven different stages of the church throughout her history. This point of view holds that the letters to the seven churches "must be a description or prophetic outline of the 'spiritual history' of the church from the time when John wrote the book."[10] This is the approach of many (though not all) of those who would see Revelation as a book to be fulfilled in the future.

That approach, though, is not the only way to understand the seven churches, nor is it the one that is taken here. The approach for this study is that the letters to the seven churches are letters to seven actual churches active at the time John received the revelation. The seven churches in Revelation refer to seven literal churches described in Revelation, Chapters 2 and 3.[11] The message to them is directly for them but has application and meaning for the church today. Here's the text…

Revelation 2:1-7

To the angel of the church in Ephesus write:

"These are the words of him who holds the seven stars in his right

10 Clarence Larkin, "Chapter 22: The Seven Churches", Blue Letter Bible. https://www.blueletterbible.org/study/larkin/dt/22.cfm.
11 "Seven Churches in Revelation", All About Archaeology. https://www.allaboutarchaeology.org/seven-churches-in-revelation.htm.

hand and walks among the seven golden lampstands. ²I know your deeds, your hard work, and your perseverance. I know that you cannot tolerate wicked people, that you have tested those who claim to be apostles but are not and have found them false. ³You have persevered and have endured hardships for my name and have not grown weary.

⁴Yet I hold this against you: You have forsaken the love you had at first. ⁵Consider how far you have fallen! Repent and do the things you did at first. If you do not repent, I will come to you and remove your lampstand from its place. ⁶But you have this in your favor: You hate the practices of the Nicolaitans, which I also hate.

⁷Whoever has ears, let them hear what the Spirit says to the churches. To the one who is victorious, I will give the right to eat from the tree of life, which is in the paradise of God."

Lesson

The first church of the seven is the church at Ephesus. Ephesus is 35 miles from Smyrna. It's located opposite the island of Samos and is the closest of Revelation's seven churches to the island of Patmos, where the apostle John wrote the book of Revelation.

Ephesus was founded primarily by Greeks from the city of Athens. Rome had made it a provincial capital and its population was large at 250,000 residents during the first century. Few cities could rival it for size, wealth, and power. Its temple of Artemis was one of the seven wonders of the ancient world.

The advantageous location of Ephesus made it the chief city of Asia Minor and it became a significant city for the Christian faith. Paul wrote 1 and 2 Corinthians (and possibly the other letters to Corinth) from Ephesus around AD 57. John likely wrote his gospel and 1, 2, and 3 John while pastoring the church at Ephesus no later than AD 90.

Ephesus was an important center of commerce. It maintained an artificial harbor accessible to the largest ships. The city stood at the entrance of a valley that reached far into the province. It was also connected via highways to other important cities in the region. The ease of traveling to Ephesus, either by land or sea, made it the most accessible populated destination in Asia.

Commendation On Doing The Right Thing

The angel or messenger to the church at Ephesus was given a message. Verse 1 indicates the one sending it. "These are the words of him who holds the seven stars in his right hand and walks among the seven golden lampstands." We've seen that description before (in the previous chapter) and we know who it is. Jesus Christ, the powerful, glorious, and victorious king, has a message for the church at Ephesus.

What is that message? It starts focusing on the positive. "I know your deeds, your hard work, and your perseverance. I know that you cannot tolerate wicked people, that you have tested those who claim to be apostles but are not and have found them false. You have persevered and have endured hardships for my name and have not grown weary" (Revelation 2:2-3).

The church at Ephesus worked hard and tried to do the right thing, even when there was a lot of wrong around them. The Temple of Artemis at Ephesus was known throughout the ancient world for its temple prostitutes and hedonistic celebrations.[12] The moral climate in Ephesus was challenging, but the Ephesian Christians were doing their best not to surrender to the immorality surrounding them.

Living a pure life was a challenge for the Ephesians and it is for us, too. According to a Gallup poll conducted in May 2018, 49% of Americans say the state of moral values in the US is "poor." Meanwhile, 37 % of US adults say moral values are "only fair" and 14 % say they are "excellent" or "good."[13] I appreciate the poll, but I'm sure that most of us don't need a poll to know how moral values have corroded in our culture. Sexual sin, selfishness, greed, hate, anger, pride, and a host of other vices saturate our society.

Elisabeth Elliot once said, "If your goal is purity of heart, be

12 "Ancient City of Ephesus", All About Archaeology. https://www.allaboutarchaeology.org/ancient-city-of-ephesus-faq.htm.
13 Andy Berges, "America's Moral Compass Continues to Decay: A Column", USA Today, January 31, 2019. https://www.delmarvanow.com/story/opinion/2019/01/31/americas-moral-compass-continues-decay-column/2722011002/.

prepared to be thought very odd."[14]

Perhaps an even greater challenge for the church at Ephesus was the push to compromise the truth. The Ephesians, though, were dedicated. They knew and held to the right teaching. They weren't swayed by false teachers.

The church in Ephesus was planted by Paul during a brief visit. This congregation was nurtured by Paul's co-laborers Priscilla and Aquila, then by Apollos (Acts 18:19-28). Paul subsequently returned to Ephesus for a three-year ministry, marked by the victory of Christ's gospel and Spirit over demonic powers and the entrenched commercial interests surrounding the city's world-famous temple of Artemis (Acts 19:1–41).

After saying good-bye to the Ephesian elders, Paul summoned them to be vigilant to protect God's sheep from "fierce wolves" and false shepherds (Acts 20:29–30 ESV). Writing from prison, Paul summoned this church to "unity of the faith and of the knowledge of the Son of God," a maturity that would enable them to stand firm against "human cunning, by craftiness in deceitful schemes" (Ephesians 4:13-14 NRSV). The apostle insisted that the church exercise discernment: "Let no one deceive you with empty words" (Ephesians 5:6). Holding to the truth mattered.

The Federal Reserve has a lot of material online about how to spot a counterfeit bill. It seems counterfeiters are actively trying to fool people and trick them into taking counterfeit cash. Giving practical advice to the retailer, the Federal Reserve says, "The best way to determine whether a note is genuine is to rely on the security features, such as the watermark and security thread."[15]

There are certain things a merchant must know to look for to determine what is real and what's fake. It's the same for Christians, too. The Ephesian Christians give us a good example regarding holding on to truth. They knew what was true. They'd been taught by Paul and subsequently by others. They were

---

14 Elisabeth Elliot, "20 Christian Quotes About Purity", What Christians Want to Know. https://www.whatchristianswanttoknow.com/20-christian-quotes-about-purity/.
15 Board of Governors of the Federal Reserve System, "How Do I Determine if a Banknote is Genuine? What Should I do if I Think I Have a Counterfeit Note?" Federal Reserve. https://www.federalreserve.gov/faqs/currency_12597.htm.

aware of the false teaching around them and they were quick to reject it.

Verse 6 is also part of the commendation. Jesus Christ said, "But you have this in your favor: You hate the practices of the Nicolaitans, which I also hate." This comes after the challenge (which we'll see shortly) but is an affirmation of the Ephesians' desire to maintain purity.

Just who are these Nicolaitans? The name itself may be derived from two words which mean "victory" (*nikos*) and "people" (*laos*), thus the idea of their consumption or overpowering of the people. They advocated an unhealthy compromise with pagan society and the idolatrous culture of Ephesus.[16] The Nicolaitans encouraged both spiritual idolatry and sexual immorality. Balaam was a prototype of those who promote compromise with the world in idolatry and immorality (see Jude 11 and 2 Peter 2:15). The Nicolaitans, in a Balaam fashion, taught that freedom in Christ granted them a blank check to sin.

Compromise with the world. It's not something that any Christian or church would willingly do, but it happens. We've seen the result of it. The church's witness is muted, and her impact is lessened. She is no longer the bride of Christ, but is simply another organization of men and women. How does that happen? I suppose there are lots of answers to that, but let me suggest three reasons.

First, there is a strong desire in our current culture to not judge others. If the church takes a stance on right and wrong, then she runs the risk of being labeled as "judgmental" or "intolerant." There's not a worse descriptor that a person or group can be called today than to be called "intolerant." Churches have shied away from calling out sin because of this fear.

Second, there is a push for churches to be relevant. To be relevant is to be able to connect with the culture. There's nothing wrong with being relevant. In fact, there's a lot right with it. However, relevance can't come at the expense of righteousness.

---

16 Sam Storms, "Ten Things You Should Know About the Nicolaitans", Enjoying God (blog). https://www.samstorms.org/enjoying-god-blog/post/10-things-you-should-know-about-the-nicolaitans.

Dear Church

If we believe the Bible to be relevant to all people throughout all times, then we just need to preach and teach the Bible. Our methodology might change (musically, sanctuary design, length of sermons), but the message never changes. Relevancy doesn't come from a diminished Christian faith.

The third one is not a revolutionary thought, but it's real. There's a temptation to sin. We know what the right thing to do is. We know what God wants, but sometimes we simply ignore it and do what we want. That happens to individuals and to churches. How many times has sin derailed a thriving ministry?

The Ephesian Christians hated sin and would not compromise, and we shouldn't either. They would not tolerate the teachings or practices of the Nicolaitans. They resisted any and every urge to give in to the world around them. They were hardened to that.

Challenge About Doing The Wrong Thing

There was a grievance, though, against this church. "Yet I hold this against you: You have forsaken the love you had at first."(Revelation 2:4) Just what is this challenge saying?

Paul wrote the book of Ephesians about thirty years earlier and mentioned their love for one another (1:15-16). He concluded the letter with a blessing on those "who love our Lord Jesus Christ with an undying love" (Ephesians 6:24). As we read in Revelation, their love has waned, but which one: love for one another, or love for Jesus or maybe love for both?

I think the answer is likely a combination of both. This church had a passion to remain pure in the middle of a depraved society and a desire to hang on to the truth despite having so much false teaching around them. It seems as if this determination hardened them, in good ways (not yielding to temptation) and in bad ways (not bearing up with or showing grace to one another). It may be that Jesus is telling them, "How can you say you love me when you don't show love for one another? You can't love me if you don't love each other."

Without love, they had nothing to back up their determined stand for truth and righteousness. Without backup, they were lacking.

When 67-year-old carpenter Russell Herman died in 1994, his will was astonishing. He called for more than two billion dollars for the city of East St. Louis, another billion and a half for the state of Illinois, two and a half billion for the national forest system, and to top off the list, Herman left six trillion dollars to the government to help pay off the national debt.

That sounds amazingly generous, but there was a small problem — Herman's only asset when he died was a 1983 Oldsmobile. He made grand announcements, but there was no real generosity involved. His promises were empty and meaningless because there was nothing to back them up.[17]

There was nothing to back them up; that's a phrase that stings. I didn't know Russell Herman, but that story rings a bit sad to me. Even sadder, though, is that there are lots of Christians who were once passionate and dedicated to serving Jesus and ministering to those around them who have lost that love. They might still be going through the motions, but there is nothing there to back them up.

What did Jesus Christ tell the church at Ephesus to do? He told them, "Consider how far you have fallen! Repent and do the things you did at first."(Revelation 2:5) Notice what he didn't say. He didn't say, "Loosen up a little on the truth stuff." He didn't say, "Lighten up on the morals thing. Just fit in to your community a bit more." They weren't wrong in holding to the truth or retaining purity. There's likely a lesson there for the church of today.

He told them first to "consider how far they've fallen." He was challenging them to remember what they used to be and what they used to do. He then added, "Repent and do the things you did at first." The challenge for this church is to humbly turn to the Lord, seek his forgiveness for becoming hardened, and then allow the Holy Spirit to rekindle the love that used to burn in them. The whole of the challenge can be summed up as remember, repent, and rekindle.

17 Wes Smith, "Will Power", Chicago Tribune, June 13, 1995. https://www.chicagotribune. com/news/ct-xpm-1995-06-13-9506130010-story.html.

Warning And Promise

The second part of verse 5 notes the warning that Jesus gave this church. He said, "If you do not repent, I will come to you and remove your lampstand from its place." Jesus' words here were direct. If they didn't repent and allow that love to be reignited, then he would remove their lampstand from its place. This means that the church would lose her influence and impact in their community. They would cease to be the church. (Revelation 2:9)

There's also a promise given at the end of verse 7. "To the one who is victorious, I will give the right to eat from the tree of life, which is in the paradise of God."

The tree of life is something we've seen before. We first see it in Genesis 3:22 where it is in Eden. Ezekiel and Proverbs both reference the tree of life. The last time we see it is in Revelation 22:2.

What does this promise mean? As we examine the scriptural record, it seems clear that this was a real tree. The promise here, though, is greater than eating fruit from that tree, as awesome as that sounds! The tree of life is a means to a higher and more exalted end. Its fruit doesn't likely give eternal life. Only Jesus Christ does that. It seems to be a wonderful description of the reality of living forever the presence of the Father and the Son. It is the tangible reminder of a restored relationship, lost in Eden, but regained in Jesus Christ.

Summary

> **Who Is Writing?** — These are the words of him who holds the seven stars in his right hand and walks among the seven golden lampstands.

Positive Comments

V. 2 I know your deeds your hard work and your perseverance.

I know that you cannot tolerate wicked people.

You have tested those who claim to be apostles but are not and have found them false.

V. 3 You have persevered and have endured hardships for my name and have not grown weary.

V. 6 You hate the practices of the Nicolaitans, which I also hate.

Negative Comments

V. 4 You don't love me or each other as you did at first.

Warning

V. 5 Consider how far you have fallen! Repent and do the things you did at first. If you do not repent, I will come to you and remove your lampstand from its place.

He Who Overcomes

V. 7 To everyone who is victorious I will give fruit from the tree of life in the paradise of God.

Note this: The one who hears is called to obey.

Discussion Questions

1.   The one who holds the seven stars and walks among the seven lampstands (Jesus) addresses the church in Ephesus in some positive ways. What positive things might he say about your church? Your family? Your own personal walk?

2.   The church at Ephesus worked hard and endured difficulty. Why is that hard for us to do today? In what ways can we "work hard" for the Lord in our culture? What do we have to "patiently endure?"

3. Jesus had some negative things to say about the Christians in Ephesus, too. What criticisms would he make of your church? Your family? Your life? What can you do to do better?

4. The church at Ephesus was discerning regarding false teachers and the Nicolaitans. How do you show discernment? How can a Christian be discerning?

5. The Ephesian Christians stopped loving (root word "agape"). What is it that causes our love for the Lord and for others to diminish? What can we do about it?

6. There were some in Ephesus (Nicolaitans) who taught and promoted compromise with their culture. In what ways is the church today pushed to compromise? What steps can we take to avoid compromising with the world around us?

7. The promise of whomever overcomes in this church is to eat from the tree of life in the paradise of God. Literally, they will live forever in God's presence. That's an awesome promise. How do you think the Ephesian Christians might have heard this? How does it impact you today?

Prayer Focus: Pray that you and your church stay faithful to the Lord in every way and that you can love the Lord and others as Jesus would have you do.

Lesson 3

Letter To The Church At Smyrna: The Persecuted Church

The church faces persecution in many parts of the world today. Sarah Cunningham writes about a situation in Nigeria that's heartbreaking. Here's the story.

> Imagine you live in Nigeria… and your family was driven out of your village by violent Boko Haram extremists. Thankfully, after days of travel, you and your children finally reach a relief camp designed to assist displaced people. Tired and hungry, you join the line of families waiting for food. But as you reach the front of the line, your relief changes to disappointment.
>
> "This relief is not for Christians." The person dispersing the food says flatly, "The food is not for *arne* people." Arne means pagan. And if you're not a Muslim, you're considered a pagan.
>
> Soon, you learn the camp itself is also segregated — Muslims are housed in one area and Christians in another. In addition to being ineligible for food rations, you are also informed that Christians are not allowed to gather for worship. There will be no church for Christians encamped here.[18]

The situation in Nigeria was tough for Christians. They had no place to go and no food. It's no wonder they were discouraged and in despair.

Discouragement and despair are traveling companions that

18 Sarah Cunningham, "Believers in Nigeria Face Famine & Discrimination in Refugee Camps", Open Doors, June 16, 2017. https://www.opendoorsusa.org/christian-persecution/stories/believers-nigeria-face-famine-discrimination-refugee-camps/.

often visit Christians, leaving them weary and frustrated.

William Wilberforce was one of the leading Christians who helped end slavery and the slave trade in England. It was a struggle and there were setbacks. One night, in the late 1790s, he was particularly discouraged. Tired and frustrated, he opened his Bible and began to leaf through it. A small piece of paper fell out and fluttered to the floor. It was a letter written by John Wesley, a friend and powerful revival speaker, shortly before his death. Wilberforce read it again: "Unless the divine power has raised you up, I see not how you can go through your glorious enterprise in opposing the abominable practice of slavery, which is the scandal of religion, of England, and of human nature. Unless God has raised you up... for this very thing, you will be worn out by the opposition of men and devils. But if God be for you, who can be against you? Are all of them together stronger than God? Oh, be not weary of well-doing. Go on in the name of God, and in the power of his might."[19]

The church at Smyrna was familiar with discouragement and despair. They were acquainted with suffering and poverty. What Jesus Christ tells them is encouraging. Let's dig into the text.

Revelation 2:8-11 (NLT)

[8]"Write this letter to the angel of the church in Smyrna. This is the message from the one who is the First and the Last, who was dead but is now alive:

[9]"I know about your suffering and your poverty — but you are rich! I know the blasphemy of those opposing you. They say they are Jews, but they are not, because their synagogue belongs to Satan. [10]Don't be afraid of what you are about to suffer. The devil will throw some of you into prison to test you. You will suffer for ten days. But if you remain faithful even when facing death, I will give you the crown of life.

[11]"Anyone with ears to hear must listen to the Spirit and understand what he is saying to the churches. Whoever is victorious will not be harmed by the second death."

19 "Wesley to Wilberforce," Christian History Institute, 1983, https://christianhistoryinstitute. org/magazine/article/wesley-to-wilberforce

Lesson

Smyrna was an ancient city on the west coast of Asia Minor, situated at the head of the gulf into which the Hermus River flows. It was located forty miles north of Ephesus on the border between Aeolis to the north and Ionia to the south. The site of Smyrna is the present-day Turkish city of Izmir.

Smyrna was founded in 1200 BC and enjoyed a rich history. The city received its name from one of its principle products, a sweet perfume called myrrh. This was a gum resin taken from a shrub-like tree. Smyrna is Ionic Greek for myrrh, a fragrant perfume used in burial. Many notable figures of history were born there — including the Greek writer, Homer. While Smyrna was smaller than Ephesus — approximately 200,000 residents as opposed to 250,000-300,000 — it was the second largest city in the region. While it was second in size, the folks of Smyrna considered themselves to be first regarding culture and refinement. They tried to demonstrate that in several ways.

The first of these is emperor worship. In AD 29, seven cities competed for the right to build a temple to the emperor Tiberius. Smyrna was chosen and became the "temple warden."[20] It acquired another temple under the emperor Hadrian.

Archaeologists have discovered coins portraying Nero, dedications to the emperors Titus and Domitian, and statues of Domitian, Trajan, and Hadrian. These artifacts all demonstrate Smyrna's devotion to the emperor.

Next, the people of Smyrna were proud of their loyalty to Rome. During Rome's battles with the Carthaginian army, Smyrna demonstrated incredible loyalty to Rome, at great cost. When Rome returned to power, she remembered Smyrna and the city was intensely patriotic to Rome. All this love and loyalty between Rome and Smyrna had a direct effect on the Christians who lived there at the time. As you can imagine, Smyrna was *extremely* patriotic. If the emperor demanded that people make a yearly sacrifice to honor him as a god — which he did — they

20 Gregory Stevenson, Power and Place: Temple and Identity in the *Book of Revelation* (Berlin, Germany: De Grutyer, 2012).

gladly followed suit. When the emperor persecuted Christians for refusing to offer this sacrifice, the good folks of Smyrna came down on Christians with extra enthusiasm. The Jews did well in Smyrna because, of all the peoples of the Roman Empire, the Jewish people were the only ones who were not required to offer a burnt sacrifice to the emperor each year. Basically, Rome had encountered such stiff resistance among the Jews to the recognition of any god but Yahweh, that they had given up long ago. So, the Jews thrived in Smyrna along with everyone else but the Christians, who were actively persecuted for their failure to sacrifice. The Jews of the day insisted that Christians weren't "real" Jews.

The last component of Smyrna's pride is seen in her commerce and culture. Smyrna was the most important seaport in Asia Minor because of its location on the edge of the trade route that went east into the surrounding areas. Throughout the Roman period, Smyrna excelled in medicine and science. It was home to guilds of basket-fishermen, tanners, silversmiths, and goldsmiths. Membership in these guilds included sacrificing to a pagan deity — and likely to the emperor as well. Also required was participation in a common meal dedicated to a pagan deity.

Smyrna was a proud and beautiful city and regarded itself as the "pride of Asia." An inscription on coins describes the city as "first of Asia in beauty and size" (although other cities were certainly more highly populated). The people of Smyrna were quite sensitive to the rivalry of Ephesus for recognition as the most splendid city of Asia Minor.[21]

The Challenge

Paul likely started the church in Smyrna, and this is one of two churches of the seven that did not receive a condemnation. The message to this church is one of encouragement. We see that first in the description of the one who is writing. These are the words of him who is the "First and the Last, who died and

---

21 Sam Storms, "The Letter to the Church At Smyrna (2:8-11)", Sam Storms: Enjoying God (blog). https://www.samstorms.org/all-articles/post/the-letter-to-the-church-at-smyrna--2:8-11-.

came to life again" (v. 8) The expression "First and the Last" is a familiar one. It's found in Revelation 1:17 and conveys a sense of security. Jesus Christ is there, beginning to end. The second part of the description also draws us back to the initial description of Jesus Christ. He's the one who "died and came to life again" (see Revelation 1:18 AMPC). He's conquered death and the grave, rendering them hapless against those who have a relationship with him.

A little girl and her mom were driving down a country road one spring morning. The windows were down in the car and they were enjoying the fresh air. Suddenly a bumblebee flew in the car window. The girl was deathly allergic to bee stings and she panicked and started to cry. Her mom, though, quickly pulled over to the curb, reached out, grabbed the bee, squeezed it in her hand, and then released it. As soon as she let it go, the girl started to panic again as it buzzed by. Her mom, though, put one hand on the girl's shoulder and then opened her other hand. In that hand, stuck in her palm, was the stinger. The mom smiled and told her daughter. "Don't be afraid anymore. I took the sting for you."[22]

"I took the sting for you." That's what Jesus Christ was telling the church at Smyrna. Don't be afraid, I took death's best shot.

In verse 9, we see what Jesus Christ knew about this church. He knew their "afflictions" and "poverty," though he stated they were "rich." The word for "afflictions" is a word that means "pressure" or "crushing beneath a heavy weight." The Lord knew the difficult struggles of this church. He also knew their "poverty" or, literally, "complete destitution." He claimed, though, that they were rich. How? Their wealth was not of the material kind but was a spiritual wealth that was laid up in heaven by their faithfulness on earth.

He cited the root of their struggle in the last part of verse nine. "I know about the slander of those who say they are Jews and are not but are a synagogue of Satan." The Jews of Smyrna enjoyed the security of Rome and their privileged status (not having to

22 James Hewett, "Death's Sting is Gone", from Illustrations Unlimited, Ministry 127. https://ministry127.com/resources/illustration/death-s-sting-is-gone.

offer sacrifices to other gods). These Jews initiated persecution and stirred up trouble for the Christians there. Jesus noted that they were really a "synagogue of Satan."

The first part of verse ten gives us the heart of the challenge for this persecuted church. "Do not be afraid of what you are about to suffer. I tell you; the devil will put some of you in prison to test you, and you will suffer persecution for ten days."

Jesus Christ warns them that suffering and persecution will continue, but tells them not to be afraid of it, even if some of them will go to prison. The statement is then made "you will suffer persecution for ten days." This is a challenging statement that has been discussed for a long time. It may be a reference to ten different persecutions under different Roman Emperors, the first being Nero, or it may refer to the ten years of persecution under the Emperor Diocletian.[23] In either case, though the persecution under Diocletian seems to me to fit better, the suffering the Christians would endure in Smyrna would be heavy.

The Promise

The promise to the one who is faithful is encouraging. The last part of verse ten says, "Be faithful, even to the point of death, and I will give you life as your victor's crown." Did you catch that? For those who remain true to Jesus Christ, even to the point of giving up their lives, he will give them life as their victor's crown. Like in James 1:12, the "crown" represents the glory of eternal life, harmony and peace with God the Father and Jesus the Son.

It's hard to imagine the joy and excitement that those who overcome on that day will have receiving that crown.

First-time Olympian swimmer Ryan Held won a gold medal with Michael Phelps, Caleb Dressel, and Nathan Adrian in the 2016 Olympic Games. Held swam the third leg of the 4×100 relay in an excellent time and then watched as teammate Michael Phelps, the anchor leg swimmer, touched the wall first. It was a moment of pure joy for Held. On the medal stand, as the national anthem played, he broke down in tears of joy. All the work,

23 John Gill, "Revelation 2", GIll's Exposition of the Bible. https://www.biblestudytools.com/commentaries/gills-exposition-of-the-bible/revelation-2-10.html.

dedication, sacrifice, and effort were worth it. He wept with joy at his first gold medal.

"I've heard the national anthem thousands of times before, but there was something different about this one," he told the "Time Magazine". "I just couldn't hold back the tears."[24]

If winning an Olympic medal brings that kind of joy, imagine the joy of the crown of life?

The second part of the promise is found in the last half of verse 11. "The one who is victorious will not be hurt at all by the second death." It is interesting to note that there is a Greek double negative in this verse — οὐ μὴ [ou mē]. It's there to emphasize that there is no way possible for the one who overcomes to be hurt by the second death.

What is the second death? The "first death" would be the death of the body, which many in Smyrna had or would face. The second death, though, is much more horrific. It is spiritual death, noted later in Revelation (see Revelation 20) as the lake of fire.

Summary

> **Who Is Writing?** — This is the message from the one who is the first and the last, who was dead but is now alive:
>
> **Positive Comments Or What Jesus Knows**
>
> V. 9-10
>
> I know about your suffering and your poverty — but you are rich!
>
> I know the blasphemy of those opposing you. They say they are Jews, but they are not, because their synagogue belongs to Satan.
>
> Don't be afraid of what you are about to suffer. The devil will throw some of you into prison to test you.

24 Ashley Hoffman, "The Internet is Swooning Over Olympic Medalist Swimmer Ryan Held's Tears of Joy", "Time Magazine", August 8, 2016. https://time.com/4443776/rio-2016-olympics-ryan-held-michael-phelps/.

Dear Church

You will suffer for ten days.

To The One Who Overcomes...

But if you remain faithful even when facing death, I will give you the crown of life.

Whoever is victorious will not be harmed by the second death.

Note This: The one who hears is called to obey.

Discussion Questions

1. The Christians in Smyrna were suffering and in poverty, despite the wealth of the city. How do you, as an American Christian, struggle in a culture of wealth and power? What are the difficulties?

2. There were those in Smyrna who attacked and maligned the Christians and made them offensive to Rome. How do you respond when you are maligned? What do you do when people say things about you that just aren't true?

3. Jesus Christ's words to the Christians in Smyrna seem to indicate that they will continue to suffer and maybe go to prison for being Christians. How do you make sense of Christians suffering? Why doesn't God just do something, so they don't have to? Has suffering or going through hardship ever benefited you as a Christian? How?

4. Those in Smyrna could literally be facing death for their faith. The promise to those who remain faithful is the crown of life. How does the promise of eternity with Jesus affect your faithfulness to him?

5. Faithfulness to Jesus Christ isn't easy and we don't

face the threat of death! Why is it so easy to be faithless when he is faithful?

6.   What does it mean to be rich as God sees it?

7.   God knows the enemies of the Smyrna Christians. He knows about those who oppose us, too. How does this impact how we treat others?

Prayer Focus: Pray that you will be steadfast in your walk, and that Jesus will help you endure all that you go through as you live for him.

Lesson 4

Letter To The Church At Pergamum: The Compromised Church

In the early 1900s through the 1960s, a large church in New York City maintained a powerful witness of the gospel of Jesus Christ. Many people were won to faith in him. From the 1960s to the 1990s, however, a subtle change began to take place in this church. The change in emphasis came about as massive feeding programs for the homeless were undertaken and church membership slipped from over 1,000 to 120. In the soup kitchens, prayers were not offered over meals, out of concern that the clients might resent it. It was also discovered that the same people were coming through the lines year after year. There was no change taking place in their lives.[25]

That's a sad, but familiar story. Feeding the hungry and helping the needy are wonderful ways of being the hands and feet of Jesus Christ, but if the church isn't about being the bride of Jesus, then she's compromised her identity and is just another group in the culture.

How does a church resist the pull of culture to remain true to who she is? Perseverance and a deep conviction to the truth are important in the struggle against compromise. The ability to persevere when things are tough is important. I think it's one of the hardest things to do, especially when junk rains down on us.

One day, a farmer's donkey fell into a well. The animal cried desperately for hours as the farmer tried to figure out what to do. Finally, he decided there was nothing to do. The animal was old, and nothing would work. It just was not worth it to retrieve the donkey. He invited all his neighbors to come over and help him. Everyone grabbed a shovel and began to shovel dirt into the well. At first, the donkey realized what was happening and cried horribly. Dirt flew on him from everywhere. Then, to everyone's

25 "Illustrations" World Magazine, January 26, 2002

amazement he quieted down. A few loads later, the farmer finally looked down the well. He was astonished at what he saw. With each shovel of dirt that hit his back, the donkey was doing something amazing; he would shake it off and take a step up. As the farmer's neighbors continued to shovel dirt on the top of the animal, he would shake it off and take a step up. Pretty soon, the donkey stepped up over the edge of the well and happily trotted off.

I have my doubts about the validity of that story, but I do think it illustrates a good point. When there are junk and garbage all around you and falling on you, you can't quit or give up. Look for the Lord to make a way out. Persevere and step up and out of the garbage. The church at Pergamum faced a tough situation and battle against compromise. Our text shows that.

Revelation 2:12-17 (NLT)

The Message To The Church In Pergamum

[12]"Write this letter to the angel of the church in Pergamum. This is the message from the one with the sharp two-edged sword:

[13]"I know that you live in the city where Satan has his throne, yet you have remained loyal to me. You refused to deny me even when Antipas, my faithful witness, was martyred among you there in Satan's city.

[14]"But I have a few complaints against you. You tolerate some among you whose teaching is like that of Balaam, who showed Balak how to trip up the people of Israel. He taught them to sin by eating food offered to idols and by committing sexual sin. [15]In a similar way, you have some Nicolaitans among you who follow the same teaching. [16]Repent of your sin, or I will come to you suddenly and fight against them with the sword of my mouth.

[17]"Anyone with ears to hear must listen to the Spirit and understand what he is saying to the churches. To everyone who is victorious I will give some of the manna that has been hidden away in heaven. And I will give to each one a white stone, and on the stone will be engraved a new name that no one understands except the one who receives it."

Lesson

The city of Pergamum was a great and proud city. The ruins of Pergamum, found along a windswept mountain along the Turkish coastline, stand proudly over the Aegean Sea. The remains of the acropolis are there, a reminder of the former greatness of the city that once rivaled Alexandria, Ephesus and Antioch in culture and stature.

Claudius Galen, a physician, writer, and philosopher who became the most famous doctor in the Roman Empire and whose theories dominated European medicine for 1,500 years, was born in Pergamum.[26] It was a city known for advances in medicine.

Pergamum was also a well-known center for the arts. The city's theater seated ten thousand people a night. The acoustics were so good that a whisper on stage could be heard all the way in the top row. The city's acropolis rivaled Athens, and its library was the second largest in the ancient world. Its collection was so great that the Roman general Marc Antony presented it as a wedding gift to Cleopatra.

Pergamum, with a population of nearly 190,000, was about 65 miles due north of Smyrna and boasted of even more loyalty to the emperor than her southern neighbor. In Asia Minor, Pergamum was the center for the imperial cult of Caesar. Pergamum was the capital city of the Roman province of Asia and retained this honor well into the second century. As strong as Pergamum was in political or cultural achievements, she was more famous for her religion. In addition to the emperor worship, at least four other pagan cults of the day thrived in Pergamum: the cult of Zeus, Athene, Dionysus, and Asclepios. The great altar to Zeus, king of the Greek gods, was featured prominently in Pergamum and was likely what was referenced as the "throne of Satan." Antipas was the bishop of Pergamum and was sentenced to death on the altar of Zeus for refusing to sacrifice to the emperor.

The cult of Asclepios was the most distinctive and unusual. Often referred to as "savior" in Greek mythology, he was the son

---

26 BBC, "Galen (c. 130 AD- c. 210 AD)", BBC History. http://www.bbc.co.uk/history/historic_figures/galen.shtml.

of Apollo and was thought to have been the very first physician. The symbol of Asclepios was the serpent, and a healing center bearing his name was built in Pergamum. It was a cross between a hospital and a health spa, where patients could get everything from a mud bath to major surgery. Even the emperors came all the way from Rome to be treated here, but it wasn't a normal doctor's visit. Terminal patients were not allowed. There was a huge sign just above the official entrance to the Asklepion that said, 'Death is not permitted here.' The only way a patient was allowed in was if he/she were going to get well. Patients were told that the serpent-god Asclepios would speak to them in their dreams and give them a diagnosis. It was believed that the snakes carried the healing power of Asclepios, so if a snake slithered across a patient while he/she slept, it was a divine sign that healing power was coming.[27]

The city of Pergamum was clearly a city of contrasts. On one side, it was a very beautiful city, powerful and successful. On the flip side, however, it was one of the darkest, eeriest cities in the whole Roman Empire.

What They Do Right — Persevere

Jesus Christ describes himself to this church as "him who has the sharp, double-edged sword" (v. 12). This depiction, which we've seen in the first chapter, reflects the cutting nature of the rebuke and reproof of his words to this church. The Word of God can cut through the layers of deception and lies that sometimes corrode the lives and hearts of believers.

Christ begins, in verse 13, with a commendation. "I know where you live — where Satan has his throne. Yet you remain true to my name. You did not renounce your faith in me, not even in the days of Antipas, my faithful witness, who was put to death in your city — where Satan lives."

Jesus Christ acknowledges that the Christians at Pergamum live in a dark, evil place. They encounter on a regular basis

27 April Holloway, "The Mysterious Healing Centre of Asklepion in Pergamum", Ancient Origins: Reconstructing the Story of Humanity's Past, September 16, 2013. https://www.ancient-origins.net/ancient-places-europe/mysterious-healing-centre-asklepion-pergamum-00828.

temptation, persecution, and sin. He commends them that they've remained true to his name. They have not renounced him. They have not abandoned him, nor have they pledged allegiance to any of the other false gods of this city. Even when Antipas was murdered, likely at the altar of Zeus, they kept the faith.

The Christians in Pergamum had it tough, but they persisted.

Only a fan of baseball history will recall a player by the name of Clint Courtney. He played catcher for six different major league teams over a span of eleven years beginning in 1951. He isn't a hall of fame player, nor does he hold any records. In his playing days, he was known as "Scrap Iron." It was said of Courtney, he wasn't elegant, but he got the job done. The first catcher in the major leagues to wear glasses and the one who introduced the bigger catcher's mitt, Courtney clawed and scratched his way to a solid baseball career. His ability to persevere and keep fighting kept him in the game long after his playing days and he ended up managing the Braves Triple-A franchise in Richmond. True to his character, Courtney took up the cause of underdogs.[28]

Persistence can make up for a lot of things. Though condemnation is coming for the church at Pergamum, Jesus begins by acknowledging their perseverance in a difficult spot.

What They Do Wrong — Compromise

Jesus Christ had a critique of this church, too. Verses 14-15 note, "Nevertheless, I have a few things against you: There are some among you who hold to the teaching of Balaam, who taught Balak to entice the Israelites to sin so that they ate food sacrificed to idols and committed sexual immorality. Likewise, you also have those who hold to the teaching of the Nicolaitans."

He rebuked them for compromise. They had persevered, but they had also acquiesced in some areas. He noted two of them. There were some there who held to the teaching of Balaam. This is a reference to Balaam, found in Numbers 22. Balaam seemed to have had a strong desire to do what he knew was wrong, and which was forbidden expressly by God. The teachers that some

28 Rory Costello, "Clint Courtney", Society for American Baseball Research. https://sabr.org/bioproj/person/clint-courtney/.

in Pergamum were holding to were teaching in the same way. They taught compromise, idolatry, and sexual sin. Their teaching was not that different from that of the Nicolaitans. As we saw in looking at the church in Ephesus, the Nicolaitans taught compromise with the culture, idolatry and sexual immorality.

As much as the Lord knows and understands the situation of the Christians in Pergamum and commends them for not giving up, they have made compromises that could bring them into conflict with Christ. The warning he gives them in verse 16 is direct. "Repent therefore! Otherwise, I will soon come to you and will fight against them with the sword of my mouth." We see, in this warning, the connection to the description Jesus gives himself in v. 12. The "sword of his mouth" cuts through and brings conviction, confrontation, and challenge. The Christians at Pergamum were commanded to repent. Compromise cannot be tolerated.

The promise to the one who overcomes in Pergamum is a fascinating two-part reward. To the overcomer, Jesus Christ promises, "I will give some of the hidden manna. I will also give that person a white stone with a new name written on it, known only to the one who receives it."

This "hidden manna" may well represent that Jesus Christ promises to meet every need of the heart that hungers for what is good and right. As he supplied his hungry people in the desert, Jesus Christ promises to reward the hungry in one of the spiritually darkest places.

The white stone may be even more complicated to understand. Among interpretations that may fit the context is the suggestion that the white stones, with names of the recipients inscribed, were given to contest winners of the Roman races. The white stone inscribed with a personal name could serve as a pass to a prestigious banquet only attended by the winners. This stone would have been received upon completion of the race.

There's something satisfying about seeing your name on a special list. I was a marginal athlete in high school. That meant that tryouts for any team were always a matter of concern. There were several times when the list of names of those who made the team was posted in the locker room, and I scanned it intently only to see my name wasn't there. That's a tough thing. It's hard when you aren't chosen.

I do remember, though, the first year that my high school had a baseball team. I and many others tried out. I made it through the first cut and was sweating through what would be a final one. I remember the day the list was posted. I joined the group gathered around to look at it. As I had other times before, I quickly scanned the list. To my surprise and excitement, there was my name, Bill Thomas. I made it.

That's not really an important thing, but I can remember how it felt to be chosen, to have your name on the list. I think this understanding fits the church of Pergamum. Those who are victorious will be honored. They will be given a prestigious invitation, engraved with their own, special name. Not compromising and giving in leads to a wonderful and blessed time of satisfaction and honor.

Summary

Who Is Writing? — This is the message from the one with the sharp two-edged sword:

Positive Comments About What Jesus Knows

V. 13 "I know that you live in the city where Satan has his throne, yet you have remained loyal to me. You refused to deny me even when Antipas, my faithful witness, was martyred among you there in Satan's city.

Negative Comments

Vv. 14-15 "But I have a few complaints against you. You tolerate some among you whose teaching is like that of Balaam, who showed Balak how to trip up the people of Israel. He taught them to sin by eating food offered to idols and by committing sexual sin. In a similar way, you have some Nicolaitans among you who follow the same teaching."

Warning

V. 16 "Repent of your sin, or I will come to you suddenly and fight against them with the sword of my mouth."

Promise To The One Who Overcomes

V. 17 "To everyone who is victorious I will give some of the manna that has been hidden away in heaven. And I will give to each one a white stone, and on the stone will be engraved a new name that no one understands except the one who receives it."

Note this: The one who hears is called to obey.

Discussion Questions

1.   Pergamum was a beautiful and dark place at the same time. Christians in Pergamum seemed to be willing to compromise, at least a little, with the culture around them. They had some Nicolaitans among them who taught that sexual immorality was okay. They had some (Balaam and Balak) who were worshiping at the false temples and idols. In what ways are you tempted to compromise with your culture in your allegiance to Jesus?

2.   How hard is it to maintain a faithful Christian witness in a place that doesn't seem to care? What do you do to stay faithful? How would you encourage someone else to remain faithful?

3.   Pergamum was a proud place (both of knowledge and accomplishment). They were achievers. I think it interesting that the overcomers in Pergamum would get

a white stone with a new name written on it known only to them. It would be secret and special. Do you trust the fact that God knows more than the wisest of this world? In what way is that tested? What does it tell us about God that he has a "special name" for those who overcome in Pergamum?

4. The new name is on a white stone. It may well be a reference to the Greek-Roman games and subsequent banquet. God seems to be honoring those who are faithful to him. How has God honored your faithfulness? In what ways have you seen him work in your life to encourage you as you have stood for him?

5. The "new name" seems to me to indicate a personal connection with Jesus and the one who overcomes. If you were asked, "Why is your personal relationship with Jesus important?" What would you say?

6. Why is it hard to obey God? What can you do to better show your obedience?

Prayer Focus: Pray that you and your group will be able to stand strong against compromise with a culture that inches ever closer to darkness.

Lesson 5

Letter To The Church At Thyatira: The Church Who Allowed Evil Among Them

You take a risk when you involve yourself with something dangerous. Al Wilson sang a song written by Oscar Brown that talks about that. The song was called, "The Snake" and describes what happened to a woman who foolishly saved and nurtured a snake. The lyrics to that song were drawn from one of Aesop's fables called "The Farmer and the Viper." It's a story that speaks to the dangers of allowing something evil to have a place in your home or life.

> One winter a farmer found a viper frozen and numb with cold, and out of pity picked it up and placed it in his bosom. The viper was no sooner revived by the warmth than it turned upon its benefactor and inflicted a fatal bite upon him. As the poor man lay dying, he cried, "I have only got what I deserved, for taking compassion on so villainous a creature."[29]

Compromise with evil or what is harmful can only bring destruction, pain, and suffering. Aesop was right to warn people generations ago.

Here's another humorous but pointed story that shows us the dangers of compromise.

> Winter was coming on and a hunter went out into the forest to shoot a bear. He planned to make a warm coat and survive the cold. Soon he saw a bear coming toward him and raised his gun and took aim.

29 Aesop, "Aesop's Fables: The Farmer and the Viper", Infoplease, February 28, 2017. https://www.infoplease.com/primary-sources/fables-fairytales/aesops-fables/aesops-fables-63.

"Wait," said the bear, "why do you want to shoot me?"

"Because I am cold," said the hunter.

"But I am hungry," the bear replied, "so maybe we can compromise, and both get what we want."

The hunter agreed to compromise and was eaten by the bear. He got his warm fur coat and the bear got dinner.

That's a strange little story, but I think the point is direct. If a Christian compromises with the world and with sin, he or she is in trouble. You can't keep company with evil. That's the message for the church at Thyatira and it's a good one for us to consider, too. Let's get into the text.

Revelation 2:18-28

18"To the angel of the church in Thyatira write:

These are the words of the Son of God; whose eyes are like blazing fire and whose feet are like burnished bronze. 19I know your deeds, your love and faith, your service and perseverance, and that you are now doing more than you did at first.

20Nevertheless, I have this against you: You tolerate that woman Jezebel, who calls herself a prophet. By her teaching she misleads my servants into sexual immorality and the eating of food sacrificed to idols. 21I have given her time to repent of her immorality, but she is unwilling. 22So I will cast her on a bed of suffering, and I will make those who commit adultery with her suffer intensely, unless they repent of her ways. 23I will strike her children dead. Then all the churches will know that I am he who searches hearts and minds, and I will repay each of you according to your deeds.

²⁴Now I say to the rest of you in Thyatira, to you who do not hold to her teaching and have not learned Satan's so-called deep secrets, 'I will not impose any other burden on you, ²⁵except to hold on to what you have until I come.'

²⁶To the one who is victorious and does my will to the end, I will give authority over the nations — ²⁷that one 'will rule them with an iron scepter and will dash them to pieces like pottery' — just as I have received authority from my Father. ²⁸I will also give that one the morning star. ²⁹Whoever has ears, let them hear what the Spirit says to the churches."

Lesson

Thyatira, located on the river Hermus, is 38 miles from Pergamum and 32 miles from Sardis. The name "Thyatira" means "daughter" in Greek and became the name of the city in 290 BC. The modern name of ancient Thyatira is Akhisar (Akhissar), which means "a white colored castle."[30]

Thyatira was a prosperous trading town that was an important location on the Roman road from Pergamum to Laodicea. The city hosted a major cult of the pagan god Apollo. The city was also famous for its dyeing and was a center of the indigo trade.

The trade guilds in Thyatira, for which the city was well known, were more organized and in far greater numbers than in any other ancient Asia Minor city. Among its ruins were found inscriptions relating to a guild of dyers.

Every artisan in Thyatira belonged to a guild. Guilds were incorporated organizations that could own property in its own name and enter into contracts for construction projects. As such, they wielded a significant amount of influence. Two of the most powerful guilds were those of the coppersmiths and the dyers. Today we might think of them as being powerful labor unions.

During his second missionary journey (Acts 16:13-15) the

30 "Thyatira: The Seven Churches of Revelation", Bible Study.org. https://www.biblestudy. org/biblepic/churches-of-revelation-thyatira.html.

apostle Paul traveled to Philippi. On a sabbath day, he met a woman named Lydia, from Thyatira, who was praying near a river. Lydia was a seller of purple (either of the dye or cloth dyed in this color). She listened to Paul's preaching and was convicted. She, along with her entire household, were baptized. It is likely Lydia, when she traveled back to Thyatira, helped spread the gospel throughout the city.

A woman, Lydia, helped start the church in Thyatira, now, though, the church is plagued by "that woman Jezebel" (v. 20). That's not her real name but a nickname, after Israel's idolatrous queen (1 Kings 16:31; 21:25) whose terrible fate at the hands of Jehu was prophesied by Elijah (1 Kings 21:23; 2 Kings 9:30-37).

The power and influence of this Jezebel, a self-styled prophetess at Thyatira, must be viewed in light of three facts: 1) women prophesied freely in early Christianity (see Acts 2:17; 21:9; 1 Corinthians 11:5); 2) women often played major roles as priestesses in contemporary Roman and Eastern cults in Asia Minor; and 3) the Christian Montanist movement in the same region a century later assigned leadership roles to two prophetesses — Priscilla and Maximilla.[31]

The Message

Jesus Christ began by describing himself as "the Son of God, whose eyes are like blazing fire and whose feet are like burnished bronze" (v. 18). This is the only reference to Jesus Christ using the title "the Son of God" in the entire book of Revelation. It proclaimed Christ's exalted status over the local worship of Apollo.[32]

Eyes like "blazing fire and whose feet are like burnished bronze" likely comes from Revelation 1:14-15. "Burnished bronze" was a refined type of brass manufactured by the local guild of Thyatira for use by the military. Apollo was often depicted as a warrior riding a horse and armed with a double-bladed battle-ax. This description, then, may be used to say that Jesus Christ, not

---

31 James Ramsey Michaels, Revelation (Grand Rapids, MI: Intervarsity Press, 1997), 79.
32 "Commentary on Revelation 2:18-19", Biblical Scholarship (blog), September 28, 2012.
https://biblicalscholarship.wordpress.com/2012/09/28/commentary-on-revelation-218-29/.

Apollo, is the true divine warrior.

The Commendation: What Are They Doing Right?

Jesus Christ said in verse 19, "I know your deeds, your love and faith, your service and perseverance, and that you are now doing more than you did at first."

The positive comments note this church is commended for her work and service to others. It seems in Thyatira, that they do love people and are doing for them. It's said that this had even increased. They've compromised right teaching, but the church at Thyatira seemed to be motivated by faith and love (v. 19).

The Condemnation — What Are They Doing Wrong?

The threat in Thyatira comes from within the church itself. Smyrna was being assaulted by a synagogue of Satan, but it was coming from the outside, against them. The church at Pergamum was confronted by the throne of Satan because it was in the capital city, as it were, of satanic religion. The Christians at Thyatira, though, had allowed the evil to dwell in and among them.

In verse 20 the Lord made the charge, "Nevertheless I have this against you: You tolerate that woman Jezebel, who calls herself a prophet. By her teaching she misleads my servants into sexual immorality and the eating of food sacrificed to idols."

Jezebel is not a true prophetess. As with those who claimed to be apostles at Ephesus (2:2) or Jews at Smyrna (2:9), the implication was that Jezebel was a liar. She was urging sexual immorality and eating foods sacrificed to idols. She and her followers may have been pushing for Christians there to join guilds in which they would be committing these acts. It's possible that for some of the Christians there to get work, they had to join a guild. Many of the trade guilds in Thyatira had their own gods and "Jezebel" may have been teaching that it was okay for a Christian to take part, at some level, in wicked, idolatrous worship. As wrong as that teaching was, they were willing to compromise and bring the evil into their midst.

Bringing in evil, for whatever the reason, doesn't work out very well. I read about certain kind of ants that have a passion for the sweet glandular substance given off by the caterpillar of a large blue butterfly. These ants become so enthralled by the substance they carry the caterpillar, itself, into their nest with great delight.

What they don't realize is that the caterpillar gorges himself on the ant larva. Usually, such a threat would be attacked by an army of ants and destroyed or repelled. However, because they enjoy the caterpillar's secretions so much, they become addicted to it and keep the caterpillar in the nest. They are oblivious that they have brought into their midst the predator that devours their young and brings destruction.

The Christians at Thyatira were a lot like those ants. They had, in their group, one who was bringing destruction and death and they allowed her to stay.

The church at Thyatira is strongly rebuked for tolerating "Jezebel" and her teaching. It was a dangerous lie that said a believer's freedom in Christ allowed them to not only belong to these trade guilds, but to participate in the immoral and idolatrous feasts that very often included cultic prostitution.

Verse 21 makes it clear that she was given a chance to repent, but she refused to do so. The result is seen in vv. 22-23. "So, I will cast her on a bed of suffering, and I will make those who commit adultery with her suffer intensely, unless they repent of her ways. I will strike her children dead. Then all the churches will know that I am he who searches hearts and minds, and I will repay each of you according to your deeds."

The warning was direct and harsh. Unless she repented, she would be cast on a bed of suffering. This stood in contrast to her couch of sexual immorality. The pain of God's divine judgment awaited her for her rebellion. The punishment went further. Those who accepted and promoted her teaching, "her children," would also suffer. Then, all churches everywhere would know and understand that Jesus Christ, the Son of God, is the one who is the ultimate judge. He is the final arbiter of what's right and wrong.

John Piper once said, "What is sin? It is the glory of God not honored. The holiness of God not reverenced. The greatness of God not admired. The power of God not praised. The truth of God not sought. The wisdom of God not esteemed. The beauty of God not treasured. The goodness of God not savored. The faithfulness of God not trusted. The commandments of God not obeyed. The justice of God not respected. The wrath of God not feared. The grace of God not cherished. The presence of God not prized. The person of God not loved. That is sin."[33]

Not recognizing the holiness and power of God or of Jesus Christ his son, is an act that will bring judgment. What Paul wrote in Romans 6:23 resonates; "the wages of sin is death."

Verses 24-25 are the words to the brave ones in Thyatira who've not compromised with evil. "Now I say to the rest of you in Thyatira, to you who do not hold to her teaching and have not learned Satan's so-called deep secrets, I will not impose any other burden on you, except to hold on to what you have until I come."

Those in Thyatira who had not compromised with this evil teaching are told to "hold on to what they have." They are challenged to persevere.

The phrase "Satan's so-called deep secrets" is troubling. The church at Thyatira, by bringing false teaching inside the church, gave the devil a foothold. They allowed a form of teaching that said Christians could participate, to some degree, in idolatrous situations, thus having some experience with the satanic or demonic realm, without suffering spiritually. Doing so was indulging in Satan's "deep secrets" and was deadly. Those who refused to do so were commended.

The statement that he won't "impose any other burden on you" is reminiscent of Acts 15:28-29. If they could remain faithful, expel the false teaching and continue to love, that would be enough. There would be no other challenge given.

The reward for those who overcome is stated in verses 26-28. "To the one who is victorious and does my will to the end, I will give authority over the nations — that one 'will rule them with an iron scepter and will dash them to pieces like pottery' — just

---

33 John Piper, "Quotable Quote: What is Sin?", GoodReads. https://www.goodreads.com/quotes/466435-what-is-sin-it-is-the-glory-of-god-not.

as I have received authority from my Father. I will also give that one the morning star."

The statement in Revelation 2:26-27 is likely from Psalm 2, a messianic psalm that tells how the Father gave the Messiah the rule over the nations of the world. This psalm is frequently quoted in the New Testament, where it is applied to Jesus as the Son of David and God's anointed.

The Lord is promising the overcomer that he will share his royalty and splendor as the morning star. First, the overcomer would be given dominion, like that of Jesus. Then, the overcomer will be given rule and splendor like that of the Lord's. Can there be anything more amazing than that?

Summary

> **Who Is Writing?** — These are the words of the Son of God; whose eyes are like blazing fire and whose feet are like burnished bronze.
>
> **Positive Comments** — I know your deeds, your love and faith, your service and perseverance, and that you are now doing more than you did at first.
>
> Now I say to the rest of you in Thyatira, to you who do not hold to her teaching and have not learned Satan's so-called deep secrets, 'I will not impose any other burden on you, except to hold on to what you have until I come.'
>
> **To The One Who Overcomes** — To the one who is victorious and does my will to the end, I will give authority over the nations — that one 'will rule them with an iron scepter and will dash them to pieces like pottery' — just as I have received authority from my Father. I will also give that one the morning star.
>
> **Negative Comments** — You tolerate that woman Jezebel, who calls herself a prophet. By her teaching

she misleads my servants into sexual immorality and the eating of food sacrificed to idols. I have given her time to repent of her immorality, but she is unwilling.

Warning: I will cast her on a bed of suffering, and I will make those who commit adultery with her suffer intensely, unless they repent of her ways. I will strike her children dead. Then all the churches will know that I am he who searches hearts and minds, and I will repay each of you according to your deeds.

Note this: The one who hears is called to obey.

Discussion Questions

1. The description in verse 18 of Jesus Christ is intense. It would be almost a scary sight to see. Proverbs 9:10 says the "fear of the Lord is the beginning of wisdom." His judgment of Jezebel and her children is severe. What is the proper place for "fear" or "respect" of the Lord in a Christian's life? Why do you suppose people today don't have as much "fear" of the Lord?

2. It seemed that some in Thyatira were compromising with the world around them. Why is it so hard to not compromise with the world around us? What are some things that you can do to help you stay strong and persevere?

3. What are some ways that Christians today tolerate evil? Why do you think some Christians are hesitant to expel the "evil" in their midst?

4. The Christians in Thyatira were doing more than they'd done before. Though there were some real problems, they did have some spiritual growth. Are you

doing more for the Lord than you did last year? Are you more "dedicated" to Christ now than you were then? What motivates you to give more of you to Jesus Christ?

5. This is the second church thus far to battle sexual immorality and sin. That seems to be a common thread and is present today. Why is sin in that area so difficult?

6. Jesus Christ told the church at Thyatira to hold on to the truth. He wouldn't burden them with any other burden. How can you demonstrate faithfulness in all areas of your life?

7. The reward here in Thyatira is to rule with and be with Jesus Christ forever. How does that motivate you to be faithful?

Prayer Focus: Pray that you and your church will hold to the truth and stand against the evil that threatens you.

Lesson 6

Letter To The Church At Sardis: The Dead Church

A new pastor in a small Midwestern town spent the first four days of his new ministry making personal visits to each of the members, inviting them to come to his first service.

The following Sunday, however, the church was almost empty. Hardly anyone came. Accordingly, the pastor placed a notice in the local newspaper, stating that because the church was dead, it was everyone's duty to give it a decent Christian burial. The notice stated the funeral would be held the following Sunday afternoon.

Curious about such a strange thing, a large crowd gathered in the church that Sunday afternoon. In front of the pulpit, they saw a closed coffin, smothered with flowers. After the pastor delivered the eulogy, he opened the casket and invited the congregation to come forward and pay their final respects to their dead church.

Puzzled as to what would represent the corpse of a "dead church", all the people lined up to look into the casket. Each mourner looked in quickly, then turned away with a guilty look.

In the casket, tilted at the correct angle, was a large mirror.

That's an old "preacher" story, but a good one with some convicting truth. A dead church, however funny this story might be, isn't really a laughing matter. The church we're looking at today is a church that, because of their own sin, was dying. They once had a faith, but while they claimed to be Christians, their hearts were far from Jesus Christ.

It's not hard, I suppose, to act like a Christian and the act can fool a lot of people, but you know the truth and so does God. Here's another ridiculous and a bit humorous story that demonstrates the danger in pretending to be something you aren't.

There was a zoo that was noted for their great collection of different animals. One day the gorilla died, and to keep up the appearance of a full range of animals, the zookeeper hired a man to wear a gorilla suit and fill in for the dead animal. It was his first day on the job, and the man didn't know how to act like a gorilla very well. As he tried to move convincingly, he got too close to the wall of the enclosure and tripped and fell into the lion exhibit. He began to scream, convinced his life was over... until the lion spoke to him: "Be quiet, or you're going to get us both fired!"

I suppose that's the extreme of acting like something you're not. If you're acting like a wild animal in a crazy zoo, I suppose that's not too bad. If, though, you're acting like you are a Christian when you're not, that's more serious. Hardly anything will put a church on life-support faster than people who say they are Christians but aren't. Those who merely proclaim the name without the accompanying lifestyle wound the church, sometimes mortally.

Today we'll look at a church that wore the right name and started well. They had a good reputation but no real relationship. The church at Sardis was dying, and there's a lot we can learn from it.

Revelation 3:1-6

"To the angel of the church in Sardis write:

These are the words of him who holds the seven spirits of God and the seven stars. I know your deeds; you have a reputation of being alive, but you are dead. ²Wake up! Strengthen what remains and is about to die, for I have found your deeds unfinished in the sight of my God. ³Remember, therefore, what you have received and heard; hold it fast, and repent. But if you do not wake up, I will come like a thief, and you will not know at what time I will come to you.

⁴Yet you have a few people in Sardis who have not soiled their clothes. They will walk with me, dressed in white, for they are worthy. ⁵The one who is victorious will, like them, be dressed in white. I will never blot out the name of that person from the book of life but will acknowledge that name before my Father and his angels. ⁶Whoever has ears, let them hear what the Spirit says to the churches."

Lesson

Sardis was noted for its past wealth and splendor, but it had deteriorated greatly at the time of this writing. Her greatness lay in the past. The greatest king of Sardis, Croesus, expressed himself with unlimited luxury and wealth. Sardis had, at one time, been unconquerable because of its ideal physical arrangement and topography for defense. It sat on a mountain surrounded by steep cliffs almost impossible to scale, with only one narrow way of approach. It is said that even a child could have defended the city from an attack by watching the one area where the wall could have been scaled.[34]

It was an incredibly strategic location, yet Sardis had been attacked and conquered twice! How did that happen? Sardis became arrogant. They were so certain they were okay, they simply stopped watching (3:2-3). Eventually though, the wars dissipated and the Pax Romana, the Roman Peace, settled in. Under Rome, Sardis became a center for dying wool and making garments. The city was also famous for its textile and jewelry industry.

A large complex built in the center of the lower city included a gymnasium and a bathhouse. The complex was over five acres in size and its western part was characterized by large vaulted halls for bathing. The eastern part was a *palaestra*, a large open courtyard for exercise.

Earthquakes were common in this part of the world, and in AD 17 the city was destroyed by such a tremor. The Roman emperor Tiberius cancelled the taxes of the people and rebuilt the city. In his honor, the citizens of Sardis and of neighboring towns erected a large monument. However, Sardis never regained her glory and splendor.

Sardis was devoted to the worship of Artemis, Cybele, and Demeter. Artemis, however, was the main goddess of the city and the temple dedicated to her in Sardis was one of the seven largest Greek temples (more than double the size of the Parthenon).

34 John Macarthur, "Sardis: The Dead Church", Grace to You, February 9, 1992. https://www.gty.org/library/sermons-library/66-11/sardis-the-dead-church.

Dear Church

Artemis, known as Diana by the Romans, was the daughter of Zeus and twin of Apollo. She was the goddess of the hunt, the moon, and fertility.

It is said of the worship of Cybele that no worshiper could enter her temple with soiled clothes. White, clean robes were given to those who would come to these temples. Worship of the false goddess, however, was far from pure or clean. It was repugnant and sinful. The Christians there lived among this debauchery.

The church in Sardis, mirroring the story arc of the city, was once alive and thriving, but now was nearly dead.

The Message

Jesus Christ began in the first half of verse 1 saying, "These are the words of him who holds the seven spirits of God and the seven stars." This is, by now, a familiar reference. We've seen it in the first two chapters of Revelation. Jesus Christ was identifying himself as the powerful, glorious, and victorious king who had a message for the church at Sardis.

It's also clear from the text that the Lord did not have any words of commendation for the church at Sardis. This is the first of the seven churches, though not the last, to be in that situation. He will, later, speak of some who have not soiled their clothes (idolatrous worship), but the church as a whole was not commended.

What Were They Doing Wrong?

The rest of verse 1 indicated, in rather stark terms, the truth about Sardis. "I know your deeds; you have a reputation of being alive, but you are dead." Can there be any more tragic words for a church to hear than the words "you are dead?"

Jesus Christ was acknowledging that the church in Sardis had the correct name and that at one time, they'd been alive, and people knew of them. But that was then, and now, it just wasn't so. The church was dying. It was a reality check time. It was time for them to face the music.

A long time ago, a man wanted to play in the Imperial

Orchestra, but he couldn't play a note. Since he was a person of great wealth and influence, however, he demanded to be allowed to join the orchestra so he could perform in front of the king. The conductor agreed to let him sit in the second row of the orchestra. Even though he couldn't read music, he was given a flute, and when a concert would begin, he would raise the flute, pucker his lips, and move his fingers. He went through all the motions of playing, but he never made a sound.

This deception went on for two years. Then one day a new conductor took over the Imperial Orchestra. He told the orchestra members that he wanted to personally audition all the players to see how well they could play. The audition would weed out all those who did not meet his standards, and he would dismiss them from the orchestra. One by one the players performed in his presence. Frantic with worry when it was his turn, the phony flutist pretended to be sick. The doctor who was ordered to examine him, however, declared that he was perfectly well. The conductor insisted that the man appear and demonstrate his skill. Ashamed, the man had to confess that he was a fake. That was the day he had to "face the music."[35]

Facing the music can be hard. If you've only put on a pretense of being something that you aren't or being able to do something that you can't, that day is a dreaded one. That's the message that Jesus Christ gives the Christians in Sardis. They were faking a real walk and now they'd been called on it.

Two miles outside of Sardis there was a hot springs. People believed that the gods manifested life-giving power in the hot waters. So, many people went out to the hot springs seeking life from the false gods. It is a tragic irony that in Sardis, pagan religions celebrated the ability of their false gods to give life and the true church with the true God was dead.[36]

The Challenge

In verses 2-3 we find the challenge Jesus Christ gave Sardis.

35 Wayne Rice, "Face the Music", Hot Illustrations for Youth Talks, Ministry 127. https://ministry127.com/resources/illustration/face-the-music.
36 MacArthur, John, "Sardis-The Dead Church," Grace to You" https://www.gty.org/library/sermons-library/66-11/sardis-the-dead-church

"Wake up! Strengthen what remains and is about to die, for I have found your deeds unfinished in the sight of my God. Remember, therefore, what you have received and heard; hold it fast, and repent. But if you do not wake up, I will come like a thief, and you will not know at what time I will come to you."

The challenge for the Christians at Sardis began with the exclamation, "Wake up!" They needed to live out a real, genuine faith. The fire that had grown cold had to be rekindled. The passion that they once had and lost had to be restored. They had to remember what they'd received and heard. Wake up, church at Sardis. Wake up!

In 1970, the Everly Brothers had a hit song called "Wake Up Little Susie." The song described a high school boy on a date with his girlfriend, Susie. They went to the drive-in movie but fell asleep. They slept through Susie's ten o'clock curfew and the boy awakened first to find it was four o'clock in the morning! This line expressed his angst. "We've both been sound asleep, wake up, little Susie, ...and we're in trouble deep." They then contemplated the reactions of her parents and their friends.

It is a terrible feeling to have slept through what you shouldn't have missed. That's what Sardis was doing, and Jesus Christ implored those people to "Wake up!" They had to persevere and repent. The warning would easily resonate in Sardis. Jesus Christ said he would come like a thief. Twice in their history, they had been caught unprepared. That's the kind of warning they would easily understand.

The Promise

The promise is found in vv. 4-5. "Yet you have a few people in Sardis who have not soiled their clothes. They will walk with me, dressed in white, for they are worthy. ⁵The one who is victorious will, like them, be dressed in white. I will never blot out the name of that person from the book of life but will acknowledge that name before my Father and his angels."

There were a few people in Sardis who'd not "soiled their clothes." The word "soiled," means to smear, to pollute, or to stain.[37] For those who had kept clean, they would be dressed in white. This stood in stark contrast to the white garments given worshipers of the false goddesses of the city. Where the false goddesses promised purity, only Jesus could give it. Those who were faithful to him would be pure.

Purity matters. There are some, even in our culture today, who've not soiled their clothes. One of them is former NBA star David Robinson. Robinson was a graduate of the Naval Academy and called "The Admiral" during his time in the NBA. He was an amazing player and an all-star. In his book *For Men Only*, Jeff Feldhahn described Robinson's attitude about purity.

In the mid-'90s, Sports Illustrated did a cover feature, entitled, 'St. David,' on David Robinson, the MVP center for the San Antonio Spurs. One segment described how Robinson handled himself, as a professing Christian, husband, and father, in the midst of the NBA's intense temptations. For example, during television breaks, he would sit on the bench and stare studiously at the floor in order to avoid looking at the gyrating cheerleaders out on the court.

The article also mentioned that like all NBA players, Robinson was constantly approached by attractive women who wanted to talk to him...and were probably offering more than just witty conversation. Apparently, he would rather brusquely brush them off. When asked to comment on that seemingly 'rude' practice, he said something like this: 'If any woman is going to get her feelings hurt, it's not going to be my wife.'[38]

Robinson was a role model of living a pure life. Some in Sardis had withstood temptation, too. They were rewarded with white clothes and another gift. Their names will never be blotted out of the book of life. They will be acknowledged by Jesus Christ before God and the angels of heaven.

What an amazing promise; purity, praise, and paradise!

37 Sam Storms, "An Unstained Remnant: Revelation 3:4-5A", Sam Storms (blog). https://www.samstorms.org/all-articles/post/31--an-unstained-remnant--revelation-3:4-5a-.
38 Jeff Feldhahn and Shaunti Feldhahn, *For Men Only* (Colorado Springs, CO: Multnomah Press, 2006), 174.

Dear Church

Summary

Who is writing? — These are the words of he who holds the seven spirits of God and the seven stars.

Positive Comments — None for the whole church, but a few Christians there had not soiled their clothes, that is, they were faithful.

Negative Comments — I know your deeds; you have a reputation of being alive, but you are dead. I have found your deeds unfinished in the sight of my God.

Warning/challenge — Wake up! Strengthen what remains and is about to die. Remember, therefore, what you have received and heard; hold it fast, and repent. But if you do not wake up, I will come like a thief, and you will not know at what time I will come to you.

To the one who overcomes — The one who is victorious will, like them, be dressed in white. I will never blot out the name of that person from the book of life but will acknowledge that name before my Father and his angels.

Note this: The one who hears is called to obey.

Discussion Questions

1.   Those in Sardis had a reputation of being alive but weren't. Going through the motions is something that a lot of Christians fall into. Why does that happen? What can you do to prevent simply "going through the motions?"

2.   Very few people, I think, start out on a walk with Jesus Christ planning for it to fail. Why do so many start strong and then stop?

3. The Christians in Sardis had deeds that weren't finished. They were told to hold fast and repent. Why do we sometimes start out strong in our walk with Jesus and then falter? What can you do to prevent that?

4. Lots of Christians get hung up on having a right reputation without any real actions. Does having a good reputation matter to you? Why or why not?

5. In the warning to this church, Jesus Christ said he would come like a thief. The context of Sardis' impenetrable position behind the river made the people there feel safe and secure. This warning would really hit home. Why is it good, at times, for us to be less comfortable in our walk with the Lord?

6. The positive in Sardis is that there were some who'd not soiled their clothes. They were promised to walk in white with Jesus. They were those who'd not given in to the sin around them. How is walking with Jesus Christ a motivation to not compromise and sin?

7. The promise to the one who overcame in Sardis was to be dressed in white, not have his name blotted out of the book of life, and be acknowledged by Jesus Christ. That's an important promise. How might being acknowledged by Jesus Christ be a motivation to be faithful? Do you look forward to that? Why?

Prayer Focus: Pray that we stay energized and connected to the Lord so that we are continually growing and becoming more like him.

Lesson 7

Letter To The Church At Philadelphia: The Faithful Church

Max Lucado, in his book *God Came Near*, wrote about Norman Geisler. Geisler, as a child, went to a Vacation Bible School because he was invited by some neighbor children. He went back to the same church for Sunday School classes for 400 Sundays in a row. Each week he was picked up by the same bus driver. Week after week he attended church, but never made a commitment to Christ. Finally, during his senior year in high school, after being picked up for church over 400 times, he did commit his life to Christ and was baptized.

Lucado pondered the question, "What if that bus driver had given up on Geisler at 395? What if the bus driver had said, 'This kid is going nowhere spiritually, why waste any more time on him?'[39]"

I think that's a simple story of being faithful doing what you can do for Jesus Christ. The bus driver may not have thought too much about the spiritual things he was doing, but the fact he picked up Norman 400 Sundays in a row was important in the process of Norman becoming a Christian. It's been said a lot that the greatest "ability" God wants in his people is their *"availability."*

Christopher Reeve was an actor who starred in several movies but became famous for playing Superman in four different movies. Reeve was a talented actor whose brilliant career was cut short when, in 1995, the injuries he received when being thrown from a horse left him paralyzed. Reeve was a tireless advocate for people with spinal cord injuries and started a foundation to raise support for that cause. In an interview, the man who was Superman said, "A hero is an ordinary individual who finds the strength to persevere and endure in spite of overwhelming

39 Max Lucado, *God Came Near* (Colorado Springs, CO: Multnomah Press, 1987), 133.

obstacles."[40]

Being faithful when things are tough can be hard. There's a lot we can learn from the church at Philadelphia.

Revelation 3:7-13

[7]"To the angel of the church in Philadelphia write:

These are the words of him who is holy and true, who holds the key of David. What he opens no one can shut, and what he shuts no one can open. [8]I know your deeds. See, I have placed before you an open door that no one can shut. I know that you have little strength, yet you have kept my word and have not denied my name. [9]I will make those who are of the synagogue of Satan, who claim to be Jews though they are not, but are liars — I will make them come and fall down at your feet and acknowledge that I have loved you. [10]Since you have kept my command to endure patiently, I will also keep you from the hour of trial that is going to come on the whole world to test the inhabitants of the earth.

[11]I am coming soon. Hold on to what you have, so that no one will take your crown. [12]The one who is victorious I will make a pillar in the temple of my God. Never again will they leave it. I will write on them the name of my God and the name of the city of my God, the new Jerusalem, which is coming down out of heaven from my God; and I will also write on them my new name. [13]Whoever has ears, let them hear what the Spirit says to the churches."

Lesson

The city of Philadelphia is about 105 miles east of Smyrna and 25 miles southeast of Sardis. Philadelphia was founded after Attalus, the king of Pergamum in 189 B.C., who came to that area. Philadelphia means *brotherly love*. "Its name was given to it in honor of Attalus II, because of his loyalty to his elder brother, Eumenes II, king of Lydia. Still another name of the city was Decapolis, because it was considered as one of the ten cities of the plain."[41]

40 Peter Wilderrotter "Remembering Superman: on Christopher Reeves birthday. https://www.christopherreeve.org/about-us/executive-memos/on-christopher-reeves-birthday\
41 David Treybig, "Philadelphia," Life Hope and Truth, https://lifehopeandtruth.com/prophecy/revelation/seven-churches-of-revelation/philadelphia/

Dear Church

Philadelphia was backed by volcanic cliffs and the land was rich and fertile from the volcanic residue. Agriculture prospered in and around the city. The city stood on a hill overlooking a long valley. Because of its volcanic fertile soil, there were many grape vineyards. Worship of Dionysius, the god of wine, was common in Philadelphia.

Philadelphia was a dangerous place to live. Earthquakes were common and, like many other cities in this region, Philadelphia had experienced them often. The people who lived there were devastated on many occasions by massive earthquakes that literally destroyed their city and it was rebuilt on several occasions. Aftershocks were common, and they were used to the uncertainty of living in an earthquake-heavy area.

The city sometimes bore the title "Little Athens" because of the magnificence of its temples and other public buildings.[42] Like Athens, Philadelphia was a temple warden and recognized the emperor with the title "The Son of the Holy One." This may be why, in his introduction to this church, Jesus Christ referred to himself as "him who is holy and true."

Philadelphia was founded for a special purpose and intention. It was situated where the borders of Mysia, Lydia, and Phrygia met, which made it a border town. Philadelphia was not established for military purpose or protection. That wasn't needed. It was founded with the deliberate intention that it would be a missionary of Greek culture and the Greek language to Lydia and Phrygia. The city did its work so well that by AD 19 the Lydians had forgotten their own language and were virtually Greeks in every way.

The Message

Jesus Christ addressed this church in verse 7. He said, "These are the words of him who is holy and true, who holds the key of David. What he opens no one can shut, and what he shuts no one can open."

42 Harry Kiriakodotus, "Lydia or Neo-Caesarea or Alasehir? Just Call it Philadelphia", September 12, 2012, Hidden City Philadelphia. https://hiddencityphila.org/2012/09/lydia-or-neo-caesarea-or-alasehir-just-call-it-philadelphia/.

The description Jesus Christ uses here is a powerful one. He was the one who was holy and true. The word used for "true" here indicates that he was what was "real" or "genuine."

He held the key of David. He was the one who could open the door to salvation. "The key spoke of 1) his royal claims as Lord and head of David's house. It anticipated and looked to his rule and kingdom on earth. 2) But it also reminds us of his royal authority or sovereignty even now over heaven and earth."[43]

He continued the message in verse 8-9. "I know your deeds. See, I have placed before you an open door that no one can shut. I know that you have little strength, yet you have kept my word and have not denied my name. [9]I will make those who are of the synagogue of Satan, who claim to be Jews though they are not, but are liars — I will make them come and fall down at your feet and acknowledge that I have loved you."

He began, as he had before, saying "I know your deeds." Jesus knew what was happening in the church at Philadelphia. He knew, not just the events, but he knew the hearts of the Christians there. He began by saying he had placed an "open door" before them. The "open door" noted here was likely the opportunity this church had. The city was located on an important trade route and was known as the "gateway to the east."[44] As they understood their history of spreading Greek culture and language, they would grasp the idea of an "open door" of opportunity. The church at Philadelphia would have a chance to use her influence for the kingdom of Christ.

One of President Franklin Roosevelt's closest advisers was a speechwriter named Harry Hopkins. During World War II, when his influence with Roosevelt was at its peak, Hopkins held no official cabinet position. Hopkins's closeness to Roosevelt caused many to regard him as a questionable figure. As a result, he was a source of controversy. Roosevelt had other advisers, but he found Hopkins perfect company and liked to discuss important

43 J. Hampton Keithley, "The Message to Philadelphia", Bible.org. https://bible.org/seriespage/8-message-philadelphia-rev-37-13.
44 Mary Jane Chaignot, "Cities of the Seven Churches", Bible Wise. https://www.biblewise.com/bible_study/characters/cities-of-the-seven.php.

matters with him informally. Hopkins was unswervingly loyal to the president, who in turn often heeded his friend's advice on significant policy issues.

Roosevelt was once asked about why he confided so much in Hopkins. His answer was direct. "Someday you may well be sitting here where I am now as President of the United States. And when you are, you'll be looking at that door over there and knowing that practically everybody who walks through it wants something out of you. You'll learn what a lonely job this is, and you'll discover the need for somebody like Harry Hopkins, who asks for nothing except to serve you." Winston Churchill rated Hopkins as one of the half-dozen most powerful and influential men in the world in the early 1940s.[45]

Utilizing influence in the right way can make a big difference. That's true for Harry Hopkins and true for the Christians in Philadelphia.

The Lord observed that they were a church of "little strength." What did it mean that they had "little strength?" They were a church that faced persecution and had to endure. That may be what was referenced here. It may be that the church was small. There isn't a lot said or known about this church. Acts 19:10 tells us it was one of the churches founded in Asia Minor as the gospel message spread from Ephesus. They were a church that faced difficulties, yet they had kept Jesus' word and had not denied his name. The church in Philadelphia, though not prominent in the eyes of the world (little strength) demonstrated great spiritual fortitude in obedience to the truth.

Small things can make a big difference. Consider how the first bridge that connected the United States and Canada at Niagara Falls was built.

The Niagara Gorge is 800 feet across and up to 200 feet deep with the Lower Niagara River flowing on the border. A boat ferried traffic at the base of the falls where the water is calmer, but at its narrowest, the Niagara River has Class 6 rapids. This all

45 Bill McIlvaine, "How Harry Hopkins Became One of the Most Influential Peolple in FDR's Life", History.net, April 2000. https://www.historynet.com/harry-hopkins-president-franklin-d-roosevelts-deputy-president.htm.

presents problems stringing a cable across the gorge. Shooting a gun with a line attached was out of the question. Obviously there were no helicopters in the 1800's, so how do you get the cable across the gorge?

Theodore Hulett, (bridge superintendent and later judge) suggested flying a kite across the gorge and offering a cash prize of $10 to the first person that could land their kite on the other side. Sixteen-year-old Homan Walsh took the challenge. On January 30, 1848, he won! He flew his kite from the Canadian side over to the American to take advantage of the easterly winds. When the string was grabbed, engineers then attached a rope to the string, and a larger rope to the previous, until they got the wire cable across the gorge. A bridge was built across a nearly impassable gorge and it all started with a small string.[46]

Small things can and do matter.

Those who opposed them, the "synagogue of Satan" (as it did in Smyrna), will be made to acknowledge that Jesus Christ does love them. Who is this synagogue of Satan? It may be a reference to the Jews who at this time were more opponents of the church than the Roman authorities.

The statement "I will make them come and fall down at your feet and acknowledge that I have loved you" is an interesting one. Those who were Jews, at least outwardly, who disdained the church will one day be forced to recognize that the church was indeed loved and chosen by Jesus Christ.

He then comforted them in verses 10-11. "Since you have kept my command to endure patiently, I will also keep you from the hour of trial that is going to come on the whole world to test the inhabitants of the earth. I am coming soon. Hold on to what you have, so that no one will take your crown."

What was this "hour of trial" that Jesus Christ was going to spare the church in Philadelphia? Those who take a futurist view of Revelation and see the churches as representative of the church see this as a reference to a literal seven-year tribulation period. "The hour of trial, sometimes referred to as "the tribulation,"

46 "Homan Walsh", Oakwood Cemetary: Niagara Falls, February 23, 2021. https://oakwoodniagara.org/homan-walsh.

referred to the time of wrath or judgment described in chapters 6-19. This was the same as Daniel's seventieth week (Daniel 9:27) and the time of Jacob's trouble described by Jeremiah as unprecedented in its judgment (Jeremiah 30:7).[47]

Others, though, see this as a reference not only to the persecution of the Jews in Philadelphia, but as indicator of future persecution that will come from the Roman Empire.[48] Samuel Walls noted that the church at Philadelphia was the only one of these seven churches to escape the persecution of the Emperor Trajan around AD 108.[49]

The Promise

Jesus Christ's promise to this church is seen in verses 11-12. "I am coming soon. Hold on to what you have, so that no one will take your crown. The one who is victorious I will make a pillar in the temple of my God. Never again will they leave it. I will write on them the name of my God and the name of the city of my God, the new Jerusalem, which is coming down out of heaven from my God; and I will also write on them my new name."

Jesus Christ promised to return and urged this church to "hold on to what they have." He wanted them to doggedly hold on to the faith that had sustained them, despite the persecution they had faced.

To the overcomers, the Lord confirmed they would be made pillars in the temple of God. This may be a reference to the stately columns in the temples, with which these Philadelphian Christians, dwelling amid the glories of Greek architecture, were familiar. Those who overcame would be foundational parts of the great house of God.

47 J. Hampton Keathley III, "The Message to Philadelphia", Bible.org, July 4, 2004. https://bible.org/seriespage/8-message-philadelphia-rev-37-13
48 "Revelation 3:10", Expositor's Bible Commentary on Bible.org. https://biblehub.com/commentaries/revelation/3-10.htm.
49 Samuel Wills, *The Seven Churches of Asia: An Exposition of the Epistles of Christ to Seven Churches of Asia Minor* (New York: M.W. Broadway, 1854), 273.

Summary

Who Is Writing? — These are the words of him who is holy and true, who holds the key of David. What he opens no one can shut, and what he shuts no one can open.

Positive Comments — I know your deeds. See, I have placed before you an open door that no one can shut. I know that you have little strength, yet you have kept my word and have not denied my name. I will make those who are of the synagogue of Satan, who claim to be Jews though they are not, but are liars — I will make them come and fall down at your feet and acknowledge that I have loved you. Since you have kept my command to endure patiently, I will also keep you from the hour of trial that is going to come on the whole world to test the inhabitants of the earth.

Negative Comments — None

Warning/Challenge — Hold on to what you have, so that no one will take your crown.

To The One Who Overcomes — To the one who is victorious I will make a pillar in the temple of my God. Never again will they leave it. I will write on them the name of my God and the name of the city of my God, the new Jerusalem, which is coming down out of heaven from my God; and I will also write on them my new name.

Note this: The one who hears is called to obey.

Discussion Questions

1. The location of the city of Philadelphia made it a good candidate to share the good news/gospel of Jesus. In what ways are you "set up" to share the good news of

Jesus? How passionate are you to share him? What can you do to better share the story of Jesus?

2. What open doors has God placed before you? What prevents you from using those open doors?

3. The church at Philadelphia faced hard times. Some of it was physical in terms of destruction, but more of it was persecution. Despite that, they remained faithful. Why is it hard to remain "faithful" in tough times? What can help us focus on Jesus when things are falling apart?

4. Jesus Christ said of the church of Philadelphia, "I know your deeds." If he were to say that about you or your church, what deeds would he know? What deeds might you want him to know? What deeds might you hope Jesus ignored?

5. The keyword for looking at the church at Philadelphia is "faithful." What does be faithful to Jesus look like to you?

6. The Lord told the Christians in the church at Philadelphia to "hold on." The idea here is to "endure." Why do you find it hard to hold on to your faith sometimes? What can help you persevere better?

7. The idea, to the overcomer, is that he/she will be made a pillar in the temple of my God. We've heard that expression before; "he's a pillar in the church." What does that mean? Who are some who were pillars in your faith? How can you be a pillar for others?

Prayer Focus: Pray that as you face trials and troubles that you will show the faith and patient endurance of the Philadelphian Christians.

Lesson 8

Letter To The Church At Laodicea: The Lukewarm Church

Lots of people think money will make them happy, content, and show that they are successful. I found it interesting that some of the wealthiest people didn't quite see it that way.

"I am the most miserable man on earth." — John Jacob Astor, America's first multimillionaire and richest man in America at the time of his death on the Titanic.

"I have made many millions, but they have brought me no happiness." — John D. Rockefeller, Founder of Standard Oil Company and the richest man in America at the time of his death.

"The care of $200 million is enough to kill anyone. There is no pleasure in it." — W.H. Vanderbilt

"Millionaires seldom smile." — Andrew Carnegie

"I was happier when I was doing a mechanics job." — Henry Ford[50]

Despite the sentiment that money "comes in handy down here," wealth doesn't really provide security, contentment and fulfillment. It also doesn't substitute for a relationship with Jesus Christ.

A relationship with Jesus Christ is the single most important thing anyone can possess. It may not seem valuable as the world assesses a portfolio, but it's the only thing that will matter in eternity. Sadly, some people are afflicted with what I'm calling the "name only" disease. You've seen it in the political realm.

The Republican Party is where I've seen it the most. (Though the Democrats may be forming their own version of it, too.) The website Conservative Review lists what it identifies as the Top 25 RINOs.[51]

50 Cazis, Ray, "What the Wealthy Say About Success," https://ministry127.com/resources/illustration/what-the-wealthy-say-about-success
51 Conservative Review, "Top 25 RINOs," https://www.conservativereview.com/top-25-rinos/

Dear Church

What is a RINO? It's not a huge beast in the safari. It's an acronym that stands for "Republicans In Name Only." For this study, I'm not interested in the politics of Conservative Review, RINOs or the Democrats. I'm struck, though, by the idea of someone being something "in name only." There's something not right about being something "in name only." While it's probably a political liability to be labeled as such, it is deadly to be a "Christian In Name Only," yet that's what we find in Laodicea.

Laodicea is a powerful, wealthy, influential city who thinks highly of itself, but the church there was roundly condemned by Jesus Christ. How can this be? What happened? Let's look...

Revelation 3:14-22

"To the angel of the church in Laodicea write: These are the words of the Amen, the faithful and true witness, the ruler of God's creation. I know your deeds, that you are neither cold nor hot. I wish you were either one or the other! So, because you are lukewarm — neither hot nor cold — I am about to spit you out of my mouth. You say, 'I am rich; I have acquired wealth and do not need a thing.' But you do not realize that you are wretched, pitiful, poor, blind and naked. I counsel you to buy from me gold refined in the fire, so you can become rich; and white clothes to wear, so you can cover your shameful nakedness; and salve to put on your eyes, so you can see. Those whom I love I rebuke and discipline. So be earnest and repent. Here I am! I stand at the door and knock. If anyone hears my voice and opens the door, I will come in and eat with that person, and they with me.

To the one who is victorious, I will give the right to sit with me on my throne, just as I was victorious and sat down with my Father on his throne. Whoever has ears, let them hear what the Spirit says to the churches."

Lesson

The church of Laodicea, located in modern Turkey, was the last of seven churches addressed in Revelation. We are not told who founded the church of Laodicea, yet from textual evidence in the New Testament, we can infer that Epaphras, one of the apostle Paul's disciples, likely planted it. We know that Epaphras founded the church at Colossae (Colossians 1:6–7), one of Laodicea's close neighbors. Therefore, it seems plausible that he would also be responsible for planting the church at Laodicea.

Laodicea was a wealthy city during the Roman period. Not only was Laodicea located on major trade routes that connected it to important cities like Ephesus, Smyrna, and Sardis, but it was also a center of textile production and banking. The Laodiceans were especially proud of their famed work with black wool. Perhaps not surprisingly, the church of Laodicea is noted for her wealth.

Laodicea was in the Lycus River Valley, the southwest area of Phrygia. Of the seven cities in the letters, it was the most southeasterly. It was 45 miles southeast of Philadelphia and would be about directly east of Ephesus about 100 miles. So, these seven letters traveled a little bit of a loop in Asia Minor.

The modern name of this Turkish city is Eskee Hizar, which means in Turkish "the old fortress," named for some of the ancient ruins. Laodicea had a large Jewish population and it's likely that the church started with them.

The Jews there existed amid a pagan culture. They had probably come to Laodicea because they wanted to start their businesses in what was a prosperous city. They found themselves amid a pagan culture and immorality which affected them.

The Laodicean Jews reached the pinnacle of

material success. Laodicea was the model for wealth. For example, in 60 AD, when the city was totally flattened by an earthquake, Rome offered money to rebuild but Laodicea refused it. The people of Laodicea prided themselves on rejecting the offer of financial help from Rome and rebuilt the city far more beautiful than it had ever been, and they did it with their own funds. The Roman historian Tacitus notes, "Laodicea arose from the ruins by the strength of her own resources and with no help from us."[52] Wealth and self-sufficiency were important to the citizens of this important city.

Colossae was ten miles away and the two churches were sister churches. It is very likely that the heresy that attacked Jesus Christ's divine nature and reduced him to a created being which was present in the Colossian church, had also affected the church in Laodicea.

Crucial to this city was its water supply. There were some local streams in the area, but as the population grew and developed the local streams and rivers were inadequate. In fact, some of them dried up in the winter, so water had to be brought in. The only way they could bring it in was through an underground aqueduct. Their creativity was evident as they managed to build an aqueduct and the water flowed down this aqueduct into Laodicea. Water could then be stored and used when needed.

Water in that area was important and Jesus Christ referenced it in a powerful way. In Hierapolis, six miles to the north, there were some famous hot springs. They were one of the most well-known and popular places for healing. The water was hot,

52 T Cornelius Tacitus, *The Annals of Tacitus: Comprising the Career of Germanicus* (New York: Benj. H. Sanborn & Co., 1913).

and people went there and sat in that water to soak in the therapeutic power.

In Colossae, ten miles south and east, there was a cold stream. The stream was perennially running and cold like typical water that flows from the high mountains. That water was thirst quenching and famous because of its cool, clear character.

Laodicea didn't have the hot therapeutic water of Hierapolis and they didn't have the cold clear refreshing water of Colossae. What they had was the foul, dirty, tepid water that flowed for miles through an underground aqueduct and sat there. It wasn't hot and it wasn't cold - not hot enough to relax and restore, not cool enough to refresh and quench. Laodicea couldn't provide the refreshment of Colossae; it couldn't provide the healing of Hierapolis. Its lukewarm water was useless. It's an image that lingers.

The Message

Jesus Christ began by identifying himself in verse 14. "These are the words of the Amen, the faithful and true witness, the ruler of God's creation." The "Amen" here indicates that Jesus was the one who was true. He was firm, stable, and trustworthy. You could have confidence in him. He was the supreme over all of God's creation.

He was the faithful and true witness. He was the living verification and confirmation of the promises of God and affirmed the truth of God.[53] His testimony was right and reliable. He was also called "the supreme over all of God's creation." The literal Greek rendering of this verse is that he is the "beginning" of the creation. This might cause some confusion, especially with the Christological error in Colossae and Laodicea. The word for

53 John MacArthur, "Laodicea: The Lukewarm Church", Grace to You (blog), March 8, 1992. https://www.gty.org/library/sermons-library/66-14/laodicea-the-lukewarm-church-part-1.

"beginning" doesn't refer to Jesus Christ as a created being or having been born. As Paul wrote in Colossians 1:15, this meant that Jesus Christ was the one who had begun the creation process. The assertion that Jesus Christ was created was wrong in the first century and it is equally wrong today.

The Condemnation

Laodicea is the second church to have no commendation. Jesus Christ did not say anything positive about this church. His condemnation was found in verses 15-17. "I know your deeds, that you are neither cold nor hot. I wish you were either one or the other! So, because you are lukewarm — neither hot nor cold — I am about to spit you out of my mouth. You say, 'I am rich; I have acquired wealth and do not need a thing.' But you do not realize that you are wretched, pitiful, poor, blind, and naked."

He began by saying he knew their deeds. He was aware of what was going on there, both physically and spiritually. He said they were neither hot nor cold. He wasn't talking about being "on fire" for Jesus Christ or having turned from him completely. What he was likely referring to in this statement were the waters of Hierapolis and Colossae.

He wanted the Laodicean Christians to be useful for something, but they were not. They did not possess a living active faith. Their faith was as putrid and stagnant as their water supply. Because they were useless, they would be spit (literally vomited) out of his mouth. The idea of "lukewarm" is indifferent, self-satisfied, and trusting in themselves rather than the Lord. It was the result of being a "Christian in name only."

A Sunday school teacher, a bit full of himself, was trying to impress upon a class of boys the importance of living the Christian life. "Why do people call me a Christian?" he asked them. After a moment's pause, one kid answered, "Maybe it's because they don't know you."

That one made me laugh, but it can sting a little, too. It isn't enough to be called or call yourself "Christian."

The Lord continued to bear down on how they trusted the

wrong things. They claimed to be rich and not need anything (not even Rome to rebuild after an earthquake) but the reality was just the opposite. They sought their happiness in things and their security in their wealth. As a result, they neglected the Lord and were not following him. They ignored real service or ministry to others. As a result, they were wretched, pitiful, poor, blind, and naked. The reality was they had nothing.

The Prescription

In verse 18, Jesus Christ made it clear what they needed to do. "I counsel you to buy from me gold refined in the fire, so you can become rich; and white clothes to wear, so you can cover your shameful nakedness; and salve to put on your eyes, so you can see."

They were challenged to "buy." This is a term that they understood well. This was a wealthy city of commerce, business, and banking. What they were told to purchase, though, might surprise them.

The challenge to buy "gold refined in the fire" was one that spoke to the wealth of this church. They were used to dealing with gold. The Jews in Laodicea sent huge amounts of it yearly to pay the temple tax. However the gold Jesus spoke of was different. They needed to give up the temporary wealth of this world in order to get the real wealth that was in Jesus.

The challenge to buy "white clothes to wear" was a nod to their wool and garment industry. What they had was not enough. That would be hard for them to hear, but it was true. The black wool of Laodicea was a known and valued commodity. The Laodiceans were used to having and producing the finest. What they had, according to the Lord, was inadequate.

They also needed to buy salve to put on their eyes so they could see. This would touch the Laodiceans in a meaningful way. Laodicea also had a strong, vibrant medical community that was known for ear and eye salve. It would cut the Laodiceans deeply to need something they thought they had in abundance.

Jesus Christ continued in verses 19-21 to give the promise. He said, "Those whom I love I rebuke and discipline. So be earnest and repent. Here I am! I stand at the door and knock. If anyone hears my voice and opens the door, I will come in and eat with that person, and they with me. To the one who is victorious, I will give the right to sit with me on my throne, just as I was victorious and sat down with my Father on his throne."

He began by addressing the reason his message was harsh. He said, "Those whom I love I rebuke and discipline." Jesus Christ loved this church and rebuked or chastised them so that they would come to him. He then told them to be earnest and repent. What does it mean to be earnest? The word, in Greek, is literally to "be zealous." The idea behind it was an intense, passionate, hot, fervent desire to walk with Jesus and to live for him. It stands in stark contrast to their being lukewarm.

He added, in verse 20, "Here I am! I stand at the door and knock. If anyone hears my voice and opens the door, I will come in and eat with that person, and they with me." This scene is one of the most iconic word pictures in all of scripture. Jesus Christ stands at the door knocking, hoping to enter but waiting for the one inside to make that decision. In the context here, it is a powerful reminder that though the church at Laodicea had done wrong in many ways, they could still change. There was still a chance for them to let Jesus Christ in.

The reward for the one who listens to this message is an amazing and appealing promise. "I will give the right to sit with me on my throne, just as I was victorious and sat down with my Father on his throne." Real authority and real honor await those who would follow Jesus Christ. The highest reward is still available to those in the lowest places.

Summary

> **Who Is Writing?** — These are the words of the Amen, the faithful and true witness, the ruler of God's creation.
>
> **Positive Comments** — None
>
> **Negative Comments** — I know your deeds, that

you are neither cold nor hot. I wish you were either one or the other! So, because you are lukewarm — neither hot nor cold — I am about to spit you out of my mouth.

You say, 'I am rich; I have acquired wealth and do not need a thing.' But you do not realize that you are wretched, pitiful, poor, blind, and naked.

Warning/Challenge — I counsel you to buy from me gold refined in the fire, so you can become rich; and white clothes to wear, so you can cover your shameful nakedness; and salve to put on your eyes, so you can see.

Those whom I love, I rebuke and discipline. So be earnest and repent.

Here I am! I stand at the door and knock. If anyone hears my voice and opens the door, I will come in and eat with that person, and they with me.

To the one who overcomes — I will give the right to sit with me on my throne, just as I was victorious and sat down with my Father on his throne.

Note This — The one who hears is called to obey.

Discussion Questions

1. Jesus Christ said that he knew the deeds of this church. Those deeds were neither hot nor cold. They were useless. What do you think makes deeds (deeds perceived to be for Jesus) useless?

2. Some would say that material wealth is a sign of God's blessing. Is it? Why or why not? Is it okay for a Christian to have wealth? Why or why not?

3.   Laodicea had a lot going for it as a town and the people were creative and talented. They were clearly missing something; a relationship with Jesus. That sounds eerily like some in our country today. How do we present Jesus to people who don't think they need him?

4.   Jesus Christ said, "those whom I love, I rebuke and discipline." How has that played out in your life? Discipline is hard for anyone. Why does God do that to his children?

5.   In Laodicea, Jesus is said to be standing at the door and knocking. He doesn't force himself on anyone. How does that image reflect his relationship with you? Why is it hard to let Jesus Christ into every part or area of our lives?

6.   The Lord tells the church at Laodicea to be "earnest." What does that mean for you? Are there areas where you aren't earnest? Why?

Prayer Focus: Pray that you continue to possess a real and living faith. Pray that your walk with Jesus Christ may be growing and thriving.

Lesson 9

Victory

The first eight lessons in this book address Jesus Christ and his message to the seven churches of Asia. I believe the messages to the churches resonate with churches today and can challenge them to be more like Jesus Christ. Now, as we conclude our time together, I think it is important to get a sense of what all of this means and where it leads.

Max Lucado wrote, "Nails didn't hold God to a cross. Love did. The sinless one took on the face of a sinner so that we sinners could take on the face of a saint!"[54] This is the heart of our message. This is what makes the church so much more than just a social gathering. The church is the body of Christ. She acknowledges and celebrates that Jesus Christ became a man. He lived on this earth. He was crucified, buried, and then rose again on the third day. That's the message of Easter. It is a timeless story whose impact is felt around the world.

Over the last eight chapters, we've seen a picture of Jesus Christ that maybe we haven't considered. We've tried to catch a glimpse of him in glory. We've drawn near to hear what he has to say to the churches. Now, just as we began in the first chapter, we'll close with a look at Jesus Christ and the victory he brings.

Here is our text.

Revelation 5:1-14

Then I saw in the right hand of the one seated on the throne a scroll written on the inside and on the back, sealed with seven seals; and I saw a mighty angel proclaiming with a loud voice, "Who is worthy to open the scroll and break its seals?" And no one in heaven or on earth or under the earth was able to open the scroll or to look into it. And I began to weep bitterly because no one was found worthy to open the scroll or to look into it. Then one of the elders said to me, "Do not weep. See, the Lion of the

54 Max Lucado, *Six Hours One Friday* (Nashville, TN: Thomas Nelson Publishers, 2004)..

tribe of Judah, the Root of David, has conquered, so that he can open the scroll and its seven seals."

Then I saw between the throne and the four living creatures and among the elders a Lamb standing as if it had been slaughtered, having seven horns and seven eyes, which are the seven spirits of God sent out into all the earth. He went and took the scroll from the right hand of the one who was seated on the throne. When he had taken the scroll, the four living creatures and the twenty-four elders fell before the Lamb, each holding a harp and golden bowls full of incense, which are the prayers of the saints. They sing a new song:

"You are worthy to take the scroll

and to open its seals,

for you were slaughtered and by your blood you ransomed for God

saints from every tribe and language and people and nation;

you have made them to be a kingdom and priests serving our God,

and they will reign on earth."

Then I looked, and I heard the voice of many angels surrounding the throne and the living creatures and the elders; they numbered myriads of myriads and thousands of thousands, singing with full voice,
"Worthy is the Lamb that was slaughtered
to receive power and wealth and wisdom and might
and honor and glory and blessing!"
Then I heard every creature in heaven and on earth and under the earth and in the sea, and all that is in them, singing,
"To the one seated on the throne and to the Lamb
be blessing and honor and glory and might
forever and ever!"
And the four living creatures said, "Amen!" And the elders fell down and worshiped."

Lesson

Glimpsing the glory of God, the Father, and his Son Jesus Christ is vital to understanding the victory we have in him. In chapter four of Revelation, we find John's second vision and are afforded a look into the throne room of heaven. It is a wondrous picture that defies description. God is viewed in splendor and is worshiped honestly and passionately. In chapter five, the attention turned to the Lamb of God, Jesus Christ.

The scene began with a scroll with seven seals. No one in heaven or on earth was worthy to open the seals and look inside. John said that he wept because no one was found worthy. However, one of the elders spoke to him. "Do not weep. See, the Lion of the tribe of Judah, the Root of David, has conquered, so that he can open the scroll and its seven seals" (v. 5).

Note that Christ was referred to as "the Lion of the tribe of Judah." John Gill, in his commentary wrote that Jesus Christ "is said to be the lion of that tribe, in allusion to the prophecy concerning Judah in Genesis 49:9, where he is said to be a lion, an old lion stooping down and couching, and on whose standard was the figure of a lion. Christ may be compared to one, because of his great strength, being the mighty God, the able Savior, and strong Redeemer, and protector of his church and people, and the avenger of their enemies; and because of his courage and intrepidity when he engaged with Satan."[55]

He was also called "The Root of David." Of that phrase, Albert Barnes wrote, "This expression would connect him directly with David, the great and glorious monarch of Israel, and as having a right to occupy his throne. As one thus ruling over the people of God, there was a propriety that to him should be entrusted the task of opening these seals."[56]

What has the "Lion of the tribe of Judah" and the "Root of David" done? He has conquered. Literally, this word conquer

55 John Gill, "Revelation 5:5", John Gill's Exposition of the Bible on Bible Study Tools. https://www.biblestudytools.com/commentaries/gills-exposition-of-the-bible/revelation-5-5.html.
56 Albert Barnes, "Albert Barnes' Notes on the Whole Bible: Revelation 5", StudyLight.org. https://www.studylight.org/commentaries/eng/bnb/revelation-5.html.

means "overcome" or "prevailed."[57] Jesus Christ's overcoming was not that he could open the scroll. He could open the scroll *because* he had overcome. What follows was a celebration of Jesus' victory. All of heaven sang a song of praise and victory. Jesus Christ had won. How? The song of the twenty-four elders and the four living creatures described it. Look again at verses 9 and 10.

'you were slaughtered and by your blood you ransomed for God saints from every tribe and language and people and nation;

you have made them to be a kingdom and priests serving our God, and they will reign on earth.'

This passage gives us the heart of the Christian message. It's about God's redemption, as our sinful nature is exchanged for eternal life in Jesus Christ. That's always been the plan. Before God breathed into Adam's nostrils the breath of life, this was what God knew he would do. John saw, at this moment in his vision, the joy of "It is finished." (John 19:30 NRSV).

Leslie B. Flynn shared a story that described the power of redemption and the joy that it brings.

> An orphaned boy was living with his grandmother when their house caught fire. The grandmother, trying to get upstairs to rescue the boy, perished in the flames. The boy's cries for help were finally answered by a man who climbed an iron drain pipe and came back down with the boy hanging tightly to his neck.
>
> Several weeks later, a public hearing was held to determine who would receive custody of the child. A farmer, a teacher, and the town's wealthiest citizen all gave the reasons they felt they should be chosen to give the boy a home. But as they talked, the lad's eyes remained focused on the floor. Then a stranger walked to the front and slowly took his

---

57 "Nikao", Bible Hub. https://biblehub.com/greek/3528.htm.

hands from his pockets, revealing severe scars on them. As the crowd gasped, the boy cried out in recognition. This was the man who had saved his life. His hands had been burned when he climbed the hot pipe. With a leap, the boy threw his arms around the man's neck and held on for dear life. The other men silently walked away, leaving the boy and his rescuer alone. Those marred hands had settled the issue.[58]

The marred hands settled the issue. The Lamb of God, Jesus Christ, is worthy of all glory, honor, and praise. He was slaughtered and, by his blood, redeemed fallen humanity.

Note that all of heaven joined in the worship. John observed, "Then I looked, and I heard the voice of many angels surrounding the throne and the living creatures and the elders; they numbered myriads of myriads and thousands of thousands, singing with full voice, "Worthy is the Lamb that was slaughtered to receive power and wealth and wisdom and might and honor and glory and blessing!"

Then I heard every creature in heaven and on earth and under the earth and in the sea, and all that is in them, singing, "To the one seated on the throne and to the Lamb be blessing and honor and glory and might forever and ever!" (Revelation 5:11-13 NRSV).

John was witnessing an incredible celebration in heaven. This is a picture of worship, as a congregation gathered to collectively praise and honor Christ.

We're familiar with celebrations. On February 22, 1980, one of the greatest Olympic celebrations ever, took place in Lake Placid, New York. In one of the most dramatic upsets in Olympic history, the underdog US hockey team, made up of college players, defeated the four-time defending gold-medal winning Soviet team at the XIII Olympic Winter Games by the score of 4-3. As the final seconds ticked off, broadcaster Al Michaels

58 Leslie Flynn, "Marred Hands Settled the Issue", Bible.org, February 2, 2009. https://bible.org/illustration/marred-hands-settled-issue.

said, "Do you believe in miracles? Yes!"[59] When the final horn sounded, players, coaches, and team officials poured onto the ice in raucous celebration. The entire hockey world was stunned and many people, even more than forty years later, see this as the greatest and most improbable victory celebration.[60]

As thrilling as the United States' win over the Soviet hockey team in 1980 was, it is nothing compared to the victory celebration that John witnessed. Jesus Christ had triumphed over Satan. He had disarmed death. He was no longer buried in the grave. All of heaven celebrates.

Matthew Henry observed, "Happy are those who shall adore and praise in heaven, and who shall forever bless the Lamb, who delivered and set them apart for himself by his blood. How worthy art thou, O God, Father, Son, and Holy Ghost, of our highest praises! All creatures should proclaim thy greatness and adore thy majesty."[61]

As we ended the first lesson, we end the last. Because of Jesus Christ, you and I are victorious. Let the celebration begin.

Discussion Questions

1. Jesus Christ is the only one deemed worthy to open the seals on the scroll. His worthiness is seen in his sacrifice. How would you describe the value of Jesus Christ's sacrifice? What does it mean to you? What does it make Jesus Christ worthy to do in your life?

2. The celebration described in Revelation 5 is amazing. It seems to be a time of exuberant worship. When was the last time you were engaged in exuberant worship of Jesus Christ? What hinders us from worshiping this way?

59 Kevin Stankiewicz, "Al Michaels Says He Landed 'Miracle on Ice' Assignment Because He Called One Hockey Game Before", CNBC, February 20, 2020. https://www.cnbc.com/2020/02/20/al-michaels-on-miracle-on-ice-broadcast-ahead-of-40th-anniversary.html.
60 Louie Longoria, "The Top 20 Victory Celebrations of All Time", BleachReport, June 17, 2010. https://bleacherreport.com/articles/407844-the-top-20-victory-celebrations-of-all-time.
61 Matthew Henry, "Revelation 5 Bible Commentary", from Matthew Henry's Bible Commentary on Christianity.com. https://www.christianity.com/bible/commentary.php?com=mhc&b=66&c=5.

3. Verses 9 and 10 of this chapter indicate that there are saints from every tribe, language, people, and nation. The kingdom of God encompasses all people. How can we enlarge our view of God's kingdom? Why is that important?

4. God's plan has always been about redeeming his lost people. What does this tell you about God's love for you? What can you do to be more aware of his love for you? How can you better show this to other people?

5. This chapter is about a celebration. It's about praise and worship. How does your life reflect these things? What can you do to live a more "victorious" life?

6. This chapter presents the resurrected Jesus Christ is a powerful way. How has this impacted your view of him? How does this picture of Jesus impact the way you see the crucifixion and resurrection?

Prayer Focus: Pray that you see the conquering and victorious Jesus Christ and that it impacts your walk with him. Pray that you celebrate the victory each day until Jesus Christ comes back

CPSIA information can be obtained
at www.ICGtesting.com
Printed in the USA
BVHW080738200122
626620BV00006B/524